WHATEVER HAPPENED TO THE POWER OF GOD?

IS THE CHARISMATIC CHURCH SLAIN IN THE SPIRIT OR DOWN FOR THE COUNT?

Other Books by Michael L. Brown

From Holy Laughter to Holy Fire:
America on the Edge of Revival

Israel's Divine Healer
(Studies in Old Testament Biblical Theology)

It's Time to Rock the Boat:
A Call to God's People to Rise Up
and Preach a Confrontational Gospel

Our Hands Are Stained With Blood:
The Tragic Story of the "Church" and the Jewish People

How Saved Are We?

The End of the American Gospel Enterprise

Compassionate Father or Consuming Fire?
Who Is the God of the Old Testament?

For information on ICN Ministries, or for a listing of other
books and tapes by Michael L. Brown, write to:

ICN Ministries
P.O. Box 7355
Gaithersburg, MD 20898-7355
Phone: (301) 990-4303
FAX: (301) 990-4306
E-mail: RevivalNow@msn.com

WHATEVER HAPPENED TO THE POWER OF GOD?

IS THE CHARISMATIC CHURCH SLAIN IN THE SPIRIT OR DOWN FOR THE COUNT?

BY
MICHAEL L. BROWN

Destiny Image® Publishers, Inc.
P.O. Box 310
Shippensburg, PA 17257-0310
"Speaking to the Purposes of God for This Generation
and for the Generations to Come"
ISBN 1-56043-042-7
For Worldwide Distribution
Printed in the U.S.A.

Third Printing: 1993   Fourth Printing: 1996

Destiny Image books are available through these fine distributors outside the United States:

Christian Growth, Inc.
Jalan Kilang-Timor, Singapore 0315

Omega Distributors
Ponsonby, Auckland, New Zealand

Rhema Ministries Trading
Randburg, Rep. of South Africa

Salvation Book Centre
Petaling, Jaya, Malaysia

Vine Christian Centre
Mid Glamorgan, Wales, United Kingdom

WA Buchanan Company
Geebung, Queensland, Australia

Word Alive
Niverville, Manitoba, Canada

This book and all other Destiny Image
and Treasure House books
are available at Christian bookstores everywhere.
Call for a bookstore nearest you.
1-800-722-6774
Or reach us on the Internet: **http://www.reapernet.com**

Table of Contents

Preface

In November of 1971, in a Pentecostal church in New York, God saved me from my sins. It was a total surprise! As a Jew, believing in Jesus had never been an option for me, even though I was not a religious Jew. I thought Jesus was for the Catholics! But my Jewishness was not the problem. Sin was the real issue. As a sixteen year-old proud, rebellious, heroin-shooting, rock drummer, believing in Jesus was not something I wanted. It was my *desire* to live a decadent life. But the grace of God prevailed! Jesus set me free.

The next few years were wonderful. I enjoyed precious fellowship with the Lord, spending many hours with Him. In 1973, at the age of eighteen, I started preaching on a regular basis. But by 1977, coldness was setting in. There was a gradual and subtle backsliding in my time alone with God, opening me up to a spirit of intellectual pride. Coupled with this was my frustration with hearing testimonies of things like miraculous healings of *headaches and stomachaches*. Soon I became skeptical of almost anything supposedly supernatural. This went on for almost five years.

Then in 1982, an awakening came. God humbled me, stirred my heart, and sent a refreshing wave of the Spirit. The fire was back in my life! I began preaching with a passion I had lost, fasting, praying and seeking the Lord. And there was a renewed zeal for the Word. *Through the Scriptures*, God convinced me that many of the things I had questioned — divine healing, the gifts of the Spirit — were clearly for today.

In 1983 and 1984, while teaching at Christ for the Nations Institute of Biblical Studies in Stony Brook, Long Island, I began to read about men like Smith Wigglesworth and John G. Lake. They were mightily used by God! Inspired by their example, and having tasted some of the things the Holy Spirit could do, I cried out to God for a greater anointing. And things were certainly happening — to an extent.

We laid hands on the sick and oppressed and saw some of them genuinely healed and delivered. Many of the people I prayed for *collapsed* under the Spirit's power. I was even nicknamed "Knock-'em-down Brown"! Yet something was still clearly wrong. *I knew of no one — certainly not me! — who was ministering in anything that could be called real New Testament power.* The terribly twisted victims of cerebral palsy, the totally paralyzed, or those born completely blind were not healed.

Through the years, my wife and I attended special "miracle/healing" services in different parts of the country. We were richly blessed and encouraged. We saw accurate prophecies delivered and heard exciting miracle testimonies.

But along with the encouragement there was anguish. Those in greatest need — so great that it was painful to even look at them — were *never* delivered. The Church desperately needed more of the Lord. That need is even greater today.

In the last few years, some fundamental truths have crystallized in my heart: First, the American Church (both Charismatic and non-Charismatic) is tragically backslidden. Revival is our only hope. (This is the theme of *The End of the American Gospel Enterprise*, published in 1989.) Second, the American gospel has departed in many key ways from the biblical gospel, producing defective conversions and a defective Church. (This is the theme of *How Saved Are We?*, published in 1990). Third, (to quote Oswald Chambers) if what we have is all the Christianity there is, the thing is a fraud. In fact, if God were to pour out His Spirit on the American Church — in our present compromised condition — it would be fatal. The Lord *does* want to move powerfully in our day, but there must be some radical changes first. (These are some of the themes dealt with here in this book.)

While the American Church celebrates, our beloved country sinks — into lower and lower depths. We are not only killing unborn babies, but we have begun to kill helpless adults — actually starving them to death! It is claimed that some of them are in a "persistent vegetative state." *I believe it is the Church that is in a persistent vegetative state.* Will nothing awake us from our stupor?

I am ashamed to think of the fact that Maryland, where my family and I now live, has just passed the country's most liberal abortion law. I am angered when I recall that New York

City, where I was born, recently lit up the Empire State Building in lavender — in honor of gay pride. I am embarrassed when I consider that the "Spirit-filled" Church — of which I am a part — has a reputation for carnality, flakiness, and exaggerated hype, a reputation largely deserved! I am chastened when I read the results of a recent Roper Poll, indicating that most born-again believers have fallen into more sin *after* their conversion than *before* their conversion.

Where is the purity of the gospel? Where are the true disciples? Where is the power of God? There are no easy answers to these questions, but there *are* answers. May the Lord give us ears to hear. It will be worth it in the end. Oh for a glorious Church!

Before closing this preface, I want to thank some special people: Leonard and Martha Ravenhill for adopting me as a son in the faith and helping to birth this book with their prayers; Lori Smith, for faithful and devoted intercession; Mike Murray, for a sensitive reading of yet another manuscript; the members of our ministry team — Dan Juster, Keith Intrater, Andrew Shishkoff and Jerry Miller — for dreaming impossible dreams with me; and my two wonderful daughters, Jennifer (13) and Megan (12), for bearing with me while I wrote another book. (I think the question they have asked me most in the last year-and-a-half is, "Dad, which book are you writing now?")

Most of all, I want to thank Nancy, my wife of fifteen years. She has consistently refused to believe that what we are seeing today is a reflection of what God really wants to do. She has constantly urged me to give myself wholly over to the

Lord — whatever the cost. I pray that He would take note of the thousands of tears she has shed for suffering humanity. She — and I — long to see Jesus glorified. It is the earnest cry of our heart that He would be exalted in the pages that follow.

Michael L. Brown
March, 1991

Introduction

We know very little about the gospel today. Our secular, materialistic society has contaminated our faith and confused our standards. The humanistic mind set that surrounds us has perverted our whole way of thinking. Lines drawn between right and wrong have become obscured. What is seemingly acceptable for the saved today was often simply abominable for the unsaved yesterday. We are more a Church in a malaise than a Church on the move.

We *think* we know that the world around us is decadent and sinful, yet we seem to fit right in. For the most part, we take no outward stand for righteousness; when we do speak and act, we seem more obnoxious than convicting. If we totally break with our defiled environment, we become irrelevant oddities. If we try to shine the light in the midst of the filth, we generally get snuffed out — if not downright dirty.

We *think* we know that our unsaved neighbors and family members are on the edge of hopeless destruction, yet this thought carries little or no weight in our lives. It hardly affects us in practical day-to-day terms. The very idea of *weeping for the lost* seems more like a pious, somewhat unobtainable — not to mention outdated — thought, rather than an all consuming *truth*. We tell our neighbors about the Lord and they say, "That's nice," and that's as far as it goes! There is no persecution and there is no power. Instead, children of the world and children of God coexist in cordial peace. Distinctions have been blurred. How do we break out of the rut?

We *think* we know that the promises of God are sure and His power is great, yet we are encumbered by a great cloud of unbelief and enveloped by a shroud of doubt. What we see with our natural eyes affects us much more than what we believe in our hearts. We have more faith in human doctors than in the divine Physician. To receive and retain a significant healing often requires an almost Herculean effort of perseverance in faith or else what seems like a random manifestation of a spiritual gift (something akin to hitting the divine healing lottery). Even when it comes to trusting the Lord with our finances, we will more readily place our confidence in credit cards and loans than in sacrificial giving and supernatural blessing. We are more in tune with our senses than with the Spirit.

How real is eternity to us? How real is the Lord's return? How real is the coming universal judgment? How real is GOD in our lives? Do His standards and words really determine what we do and do not do, or is it religious tradition and spiritual habit that shape our thinking?

" 'O unbelieving and perverse generation,' Jesus [said], 'How long shall I stay with you? How long shall I put up with you?' " (Matt. 17:17). This applies to our sophisticated, technological *and unbelieving generation*, with one glaring exception: We have not had the privilege of witnessing the mighty works of the Son of God in our midst!

Let me say it again: We know very little about the gospel today. We share our testimonies with our friends and co-workers. We get people to pray the sinner's prayer and then we bring them to our discipleship classes. But so many times we fail to see real conversion, deep transformation, and genuine *salvation*. How many people are pursuing *us* — their hearts shattered with conviction, their self-confidence utterly destroyed, their absolute need totally apparent — with a cry of, "Save me or I perish!" on their lips?

How many of the new breed of "born-again believers" can relate to the immortal words of Augustus Toplady?

> "Rock of Ages cleft for me,
> let me hide myself in Thee;
> let the water and the blood,
> from Thy riven side
> which flowed,
> be of sin the double cure,
> save me from its guilt
> and power."

Does the gospel we preach today cause sinners — let alone saints — to echo this verse?

> "Nothing in my hand I bring,
> simply to Thy
> cross I cling;
> naked come to Thee for dress;
> helpless, look to Thee
> for grace;
> foul, I to the fountain fly,
> wash me, Savior, or I die!"

When revival broke out in years past, the Church was given a glimpse of what New Testament preaching and living were all about. The Spirit was powerfully at work. People came flocking for miles to hear the message of the cross and left the meetings crucified to the world. It was not just human words that were spoken! Sometimes the sick and afflicted would be carried for miles on stretchers — later to walk and jump home with joy. The kingdom of God was near.

In those days, when the gospel was being *experienced* firsthand, the needs of mankind became so real. The burden of the Lord became so pronounced. Outstanding collegians gave up their bright futures and presented themselves to mission boards saying, "We're leaving all for the glory of God and the sake of the heathen." Ministries to the poor sprang up everywhere overnight. Sacrifice became a natural way of life. Faith became a normal way of thinking. Flaming evangelists reached out to, and redeemed, the lowest and worst sinners they could find. *The Bible was a living Book.*

But today, when we experience so little divine visitation, when we are so accustomed to a flesh-empowered, media-dependent message, when all we seem to hear are *promises* about the "coming great revival," when we can't find it in ourselves to make another pilgrimmage to one more hyped-up miracle rally, discouragement has begun to set in.

Let me say it once more: We know very little about the gospel today. We know very little about sweeping moves of the Spirit. In fact, we know little about Jesus Himself. If He were living in our country, where would we find Him? In our churches? At our big conferences? On radio or television? On the street? In prison? In the bars? How would He be written up by our leading Christian periodicals? And how would our society react to Him? (Compare this with how our society reacts to us.) What would our neighbors think of Him? What would they think of *us* if we walked with Him? We are supposed to be walking with Him now!

Would following Him have drastic consequences for us? Would it mean upheaval and change? If He spent one week with us in our homes (I'm speaking to *believers*) and then said to *each of us*, "Follow Me!" would we be willing? Would we be able? Would following Jesus (we *already* claim to be His disciples) require a far greater alteration of our lifestyles than the change required of us when we first got "saved"? Which would demand a more radical transformation: changing from a sinner to a 1990's saint, or changing from a 1990's saint to a real disciple of the Lord? Something is terribly wrong. Only God can set it right again.

I am absolutely convinced that the Church of today is not fully experiencing what Jesus died for and not yet becoming what He prayed for. There is something infinitely *more* and completely *other* than what we are walking in today. There is a power, a purity, an authority, an anointing, A GLORY, that we have barely touched. The Lord is coming for a beautiful Bride. There is much preparation, restoration and reformation still to take place.

Jesus taught that "whoever wants to save his life will lose it, but whoever loses his life for Me will find it." HE is the pearl of great price. "What good will it be for a man if he gains the whole world, yet forfeits his soul? Or what can a man give in exchange for his soul? For the Son of Man is going to come in His Father's glory with His angels, and then He will reward each person according to what he has done" (Matt. 16:25-27). This calls for total reorientation. This calls for new priorities and purposes. Our lives are not our own. We will give an account.

Paul was a man possessed by the living God:
"I have been crucified with Christ [he said,] and I no longer live, but Christ lives in me. The life I live in the

body, I live by faith in the Son of God, who loved me and gave Himself for me" (Gal. 2:20).

He bore on his body the very marks of the Lord (Gal. 6:17). He was branded a disciple for life.

But this call to total surrender and radical commitment is not just for the supersaints. *All of us* were "buried with Him through baptism into death in order that, just as Christ was raised from the dead through the glory of the Father, we too may live a new life" (Rom. 6:4). The old ways should be a thing of the past:

"For [we] died, and [our] life is now hidden with Christ in God ... [so] our citizenship is in heaven. And we eagerly await a Savior from there, the Lord Jesus Christ, who, by the power that enables Him to bring everything under His control, will transform our lowly bodies so that they will be like His glorious body" (Col. 3:3; Phil. 3:20-21).

That is a vision worth living for. That is a hope worth dying for. That is the goal of our faith. That is the future we await.

There is much glory in store for God's people. But it is not just reserved for the world to come! There is a glory for the saints *in this life,* but we must set a new course if we are to see it in our day. We must be honest with ourselves. The road before us is difficult and the task before us demanding. There are many hard questions to be asked and much soul searching to be done. Some of the answers are painful and disturbing. Some of the revelations are unnerving and alarming. But do we really have any choice? Can we continue to go on with the show? How much more disappointment can we bear? Will we allow our generation also to come and go, bequeathing only frustration to our children?

We must follow the path of truth wherever it takes us. We must keep our eyes stayed on our Almighty Lord and our hearts fixed firmly on His faithful love. *He* will not let us down. "His dominion is an everlasting dominion that will not pass away, and His kingdom is one that will never be destroyed" (Dan. 2:14). He will have His ultimate way in the earth. Can He have His way in you and me? It's time to begin the journey.

Restore Your glory, O Lord!

Chapter One

An Outpouring Could Be Fatal

There is an increasing hunger today among the people of God. More and more believers are crying out for an outpouring of the Spirit. We long to see a real move of God, an awesome demonstration of His power and His gifts. We want the Lord to come right into our midst. We yearn to see His glory!

But do we really know what we are asking for? Are we ready for a full manifestation of God?

The children of Israel who came out of Egypt under Moses experienced more of the manifest presence of God than any generation that has ever lived. All of them were eyewitnesses of His power. They saw Him smite Egypt with ten plagues while they themselves were unharmed. They saw Him split the sea in two so they could walk through on dry ground. They saw the pillar of cloud every day and the pillar of fire every night. They saw Him provide manna for them in a continuous supernatural supply. They saw the Lord's splendor shake Mount Sinai and they heard His voice speaking clearly.

They met with God face to face. The Lord of hosts tabernacled among them. They had what we dream about and long for — an ongoing visitation from on high. *And all of them died in the wilderness with the exception of just two.* Only Joshua and Caleb survived. Not Aaron or Miriam or even Moses escaped. *The presence of the Lord can be dangerous.*

Are *we* ready for a visitation from the Holy One? Could our churches survive a moving of God?

Consider the Book of Acts. The Spirit of the Lord was there! Three thousand Jews were saved after Peter's first sermon. Jerusalem was completely astir. There were outstanding public miracles, and even whole towns turned to the Lord. The name of Jesus was being glorified, and the disciples were one in heart.

But sin was also being judged. Ananias and Sapphira lied to the Lord — and both of them fell dead on the spot. Simon the sorcerer tried to buy the gift of God — and he was threatened with damnation for his guilt. Herod gave a speech and was hailed as a god by the crowds. "Immediately, because Herod did not give praise to God, an angel of the Lord struck him down, and he was eaten by worms and died" (Acts 12:21-23). Elymas, called Bar-Jesus, tried to oppose Paul's preaching. A few seconds later he was blind.

All this, too, was part of the Book of Acts. Do we really want complete restoration? Do we want to be part of a "New Testament church"?

The Corinthians had all the spiritual gifts in their midst. They spoke in tongues, prophesied, healed the sick, and saw the miraculous. But great privilege means great responsibility. Sin could not be swept under the rug. An unrepentant, immoral member was turned over to Satan for the destruction of his flesh, and some of those who sinned at the Lord's table either became sick or died. *God's nearness can have an adverse effect on our health* if we flagrantly violate His will.

What is the painful lesson to be learned from the so-called "Healing Revival" that occurred forty years ago? From 1947-1958 there was a great outpouring of healing power, unprecedented in modern times. Until that time, healing anointings were rare. It was only a handful of vessels — men and women like Maria Woodworth-Etter, John G. Lake, Stephen Jeffreys, Smith Wigglesworth, Charles Price and Aimee Semple Macpherson — who were used in mighty healing miracles.

But in 1947 things changed. All these heroes of faith were gone. A new generation was being raised up, and suddenly the gifts were everywhere. There were hundreds of "healing evangelists" preaching throughout the United States and overseas, many of them with huge tents and even television ministries. Some outstanding miracles *were* taking place. But the vessels were not properly prepared, and many of them fell into sin and died before their time.

One of the most prominent preachers of that era died of polio before he reached the age of forty. Another leader suffered fatal injuries in a head-on collision with a drunk driver. (He had already fallen into serious doctrinal error.) Another died in a motel room of cirrhosis of the liver — a chronic alcoholic while still in active ministry. Some became adulterers; others became corrupt and greedy. Although some were humble and pure at the beginning of their work, in less than fifteen years they became proud charlatans. The list goes on and on.

In some important ways, the "Healing Revival" ended shamefully. Only a few of its ministers came out whole. The others simply couldn't handle the power; the anointing of God was more than they could bear. It takes holy servants to be channels of the Spirit. He cannot be separated from His gifts. They are a manifestation of Him. And He is *totally* Holy. *An outpouring in today's Church could be fatal.*

The generation of Israelites that took the Promised Land under Joshua wanted to remain faithful to the covenant. When Joshua urged them to take a stand for the Lord, they answered with one accord: "We too will serve the Lord, because He is our God" (Josh. 24:18). But Joshua didn't believe them. He remembered the day when he heard his people tell Moses, "We will do everything the Lord has said; we will obey" (Ex. 24:7). And he remembered all too well what he had seen the next forty years. Hundreds of thousands of his contemporaries were buried in the desert! All the adults who followed the Lord out of Egypt perished without ever receiving their inheritance.

So Joshua warned them sharply:
"You are not able to serve the Lord. He is a holy God. He will not forgive your rebellion and your sins. If you forsake the Lord and serve foreign gods, He will turn and bring disaster on you and make an end of you, after He has been good to you."
(This could easily happen to us and our nation — in this generation.)

"But the people said to Joshua, 'No! We will serve the Lord.' Then Joshua said, '*You are witnesses against your-selves* that you have chosen to serve the Lord.' 'Yes, *we are witnesses*,' they replied" (Josh. 24:19-22).

And we are witnesses too. We have asked God to shake our society. We have asked Him to do a new thing among us.

We have asked Him to send us revival. And we have prayed, "Lord, come! Lord, move! Lord, act! We are ready, we are willing, we are waiting."

What if He takes us at our word? What if *the Lord* really visits us? What if He answers our prayers?

We are witnesses — against ourselves.

Chapter Two

God Must
Show Himself Holy

The ordination of Aaron and his four sons must have been the most solemn ordination in history. All of Israel was watching. The tabernacle had been erected and the sacrificial animals prepared. There was a sense of incredible awe. Now it was time to begin.

Aaron and his sons were brought forward and washed with water — just as the Lord commanded. Aaron was clothed with his glorious priestly garments — just as the Lord commanded. Moses anointed the tabernacle and Aaron with the holy oil — just as the Lord commanded. He clothed Aaron's four sons in their tunics, sashes and headbands — just as the Lord commanded. The sacrifices were offered, one by one — just as the Lord commanded. Their blood was mixed with oil and sprinkled on Aaron and his sons — just as the Lord commanded.

Then Moses said to Aaron, Nadab, Abihu, Eleazar and Ithamar,

"Do not leave the entrance to the Tent of Meeting for seven days, until the days of your ordination are completed, for your ordination will last seven days. You must stay at the entrance to the Tent of Meeting day and night for seven days and *do what the Lord requires, so you will not die*; for this is what I have been commanded. So Aaron and his sons did everything the Lord commanded Moses" (Lev. 8:33,35-36).

And then they waited. There were seven days of anticipation, seven days of expectation and suspense, seven last days of preparation. Then, on the eighth day, the waiting was over. Moses gave the final instructions: "This is what the Lord has commanded you to do, so that the glory of the Lord may appear to you" (Lev. 9:6). God would come down on this day.

Aaron came and sacrificed his sin offering, and his sons brought the blood to him — just as the Lord commanded. Then he slaughtered the burnt offering, and his sons brought it to him piece by piece — just as the Lord commanded. Then he offered up the sacrifices for the people: the sin offering, the burnt offering, the grain offering and the fellowship offering — just as the Lord commanded.

"Then Aaron lifted his hands toward the people and blessed them. And having sacrificed the sin offering, the burnt offering and the fellowship offering, he stepped down" (Lev. 9:22).

Just imagine the incredible feeling. This wasn't a dream. It was all taking place. Aaron and his sons were now priests of the Lord. They alone could serve in the Holy Place of the King of the whole earth. They had done everything in detailed obedience — just as the Lord commanded. And now He was going to appear.

"Moses and Aaron then went into the Tent of Meeting. When they came out, they blessed the people; and the glory of the Lord appeared to all the people. Fire came out from the presence of the Lord and consumed the burnt offering and the fat portions on the altar. And when all the people saw it, they shouted for joy and fell facedown" (Lev. 9:23-24).

And then "Aaron's sons, Nadab and Abihu took their censers, put fire in them and added incense; and they offered unauthorized fire before the Lord, *contrary to His command.* So fire came out from the presence of the Lord and consumed them, and they died before the Lord" (Lev. 10:1-2).
The fire fell twice that day — all in a matter of minutes!

First the flames from heaven consumed Aaron's sacrifices; then the flames from heaven consumed Aaron's sons. First there was joy; then there was judgment. First there was exhilaration; then there was agony. In an instant the mood of the nation had turned. The people of Israel — and Aaron — were getting to know their God. He was an all-consuming Fire.

"Moses then said to Aaron, 'This is what the Lord spoke of when He said: *"Among those who approach Me I will show Myself holy; in the sight of all the people I will be honored"* ' " (Lev. 10:3).
Either by sanctioning our specific obedience or by condemning our presumptuous disobedience, God will show Himself holy before the world. He will; He shall; He must. What an awesome responsibility it is to be in the service of the Lord. He will get Himself honor *through us!*

This is an overwhelming truth. People will judge God *by us,* His earthly representatives, especially those of us in the ministry. If we are holy, righteous and compassionate, then our lives give good testimony of our God. But if we who bear His name before the world are unclean, lazy, greedy, immature, selfish and carnal, we bring reproach to the Lord. So He must judge us, *often publicly*. Then everyone will know that He is holy and that He will not tolerate evil — especially among thóse who approach Him, those with whom He is intimate.

What kind of God would He be if He permitted filthy sinners to march in and out of His presence and never corrected or rebuked their lifestyles? What would we think of Him if He richly blessed arrogant preachers, people who are sometimes self-appointed prophets claiming to be His handpicked spokesmen? How much respect would we have for an earthly father who emphasized parental authority yet let his own children dishonor him in public? How seriously could we take the message of a pastor who preached holiness from the pulpit and yet tolerated adultery among his elders?

When God allows sin to go unchecked among His people, they begin to feel that His standards are loose, and the world doesn't take Him seriously. And while it is true that He will pour out mercy on those who are contrite, who really want to be free (even if they are struggling), His message is clear for those who think they can get away with sin: "These [evil] things you have done and I kept silent; *you thought I was altogether like you*. But I will rebuke you and accuse you to your face" (Ps. 50:21). Then all the records will be set straight.

When Aaron and his sons obeyed the Lord's commands — down to the minute details and ordinances — His glory appeared among them. All Israel knew that He was holy, that He would back up His Word. When Nadab and Abihu disobeyed Him — in a seemingly minor infraction — His glory appeared again. Once more all Israel knew that He was holy, that He would back up His Word. How much better it is for us when God shows Himself holy by what He does *through* us, instead of by what He does *to* us!

High voltage wires can electrify or electrocute. It all depends on how they're handled. You can't play games with 10,000 volts. And you can't play games with the power of God. Serving Him is serious business. Our carefree attitudes must go. We must carry out His work in His way, or His fire will consume *us* instead of our offerings.

When Moses and Aaron disobeyed God at the waters of Meribah, the Lord rebuked them:
   " 'Because you did not trust in Me enough *to honor Me as holy in the sight of all the Israelites* [by obeying the Lord's command to speak to the rock, not strike it], you will not bring this community into the land I give them.' These were the waters of Meribah, where the Israelites quarreled with the Lord and where *He showed Himself holy among them*" by judging Moses and Aaron (Num. 20:12-13).

Maybe the children of Israel overreacted when they said: "We will die! We are lost, we are all lost! *Anyone who even comes near the tabernacle of the Lord will die.* Are we all going to die?" (Num. 17:12-13), but they were closer to the truth than many of us today who have almost no reverence at all for the holy nature of our God. " 'For I am a great king,' says the Lord Almighty, 'and My name is to be feared among the nations' " (Mal. 1:14).

Here is something serious to consider: The Lord Jesus cares deeply about how He is represented in our country, and He is largely represented by major media ministers! Of course, there are godly servants who are seeking to preach a message worthy of the Lord, be it through radio, TV or the printed page. But what does Jesus think about much of what is said of Him by many of our well-known ministers? How has He been portrayed by some television preachers? How do their lifestyles and teachings speak of the Lord? He must show Himself holy through His representatives, either by lifting them up or by bringing them down. He must be honored in the sight of all the people.

Does Jesus approve when He is presented with game show hype and Hollywood irreverence? Does the Lord endorse a gospel that leaves out the cross and treats sacrifice as a dirty word? Is He pleased when His servants plead for money and beg for bigger offerings in His name as if *He* were making them do it? What does Jesus think of such things?

Does He smile at teaching that makes His lordship an optional extra? Does He condone those who offer Him to the masses as the all-purpose Satisfier of their carnal cravings? "Just ask Jesus in!" Then, as A. W. Tozer has so powerfully expressed it:

Come with your basket to "receive the religious equivalent of everything the world offers and enjoy it to the limit. Those who have not accepted Christ must be content with this world, but the Christian gets this one with the one to come thrown in as a bonus."

How the Lord must despise all of this. He has to show Himself holy, lest we think He endorses and condones.

What does Jesus think about the rampant immorality among the leaders in His Church? We in ministry are supposed to reflect His character! How does He feel about the division that exists among His people? We are His ambassadors to the world! How does He feel when His children no longer reverence Him, when sinners look at us and are often emboldened to sin even more? We are the ones called to be without spot or wrinkle! *Today's Church could make a prune look smooth.*

Jesus will not remain silent forever. He will not, He cannot hold back if His honor is to be preserved in our generation. When He speaks the whole nation will hear — and fear. He still cares about dignity and honor, even if we have largely lost sight of His majesty. He is still the Head of the Church.

When the Israelites were in Babylonian captivity, the Lord determined to bring them back to the Land, because His name was being blasphemed among the nations. People were mocking *Him* because *His* Temple lay in ruins and *His* chosen ones were languishing in exile. So He acted for His sake, not theirs.

"It is not for your sake, O house of Israel, that I am going to do these things, but for the sake of My holy name, which you have profaned among the nations where you have gone. I will show the holiness of My great name, which has been profaned among the nations, the name you profaned among them. Then the nations will know that I am the Lord, declares the Sovereign Lord, when I show Myself holy *through you* before their eyes" (Ezek. 36:22-23).

In our day, in the sight of all the world, He is about to show Himself holy once more — *through us.* Is there anything we can do, or will the American Church go the way of Nadab and Abihu?

This is our only hope: Those who fall on the rock will be broken to pieces, but those on whom it falls will be crushed (Matt. 21:44). Let us fall on the Rock, asking for mercy. Let us pray, "O Lord, come!" And let us ask God to be glorified among us — whatever the consequences might be.

We cannot afford to live any longer
without the glory of the Lord.

Chapter Three

Is Christianity a Fraud?

There is a sad phenomenon in the Church today: bored believers! God's children are finding the gospel stale, and going to church doesn't provide much relief. For some, church attendance *at best* offers a quick and temporary lift; at worst the weekly service is something to be endured. And outside the church buildings it isn't much better. In so many circles, so little is happening. It would be bad enough if believers were discouraged, oppressed or worn out. But believers being bored? How can this be?

The disciples in the Book of Acts turned their world upside down. When they were beaten and whipped, they rejoiced and sang hymns. When they were martyred, their faces glowed; even their greatest persecutor was gloriously transformed. Angels opened prison doors and earthquakes rattled jail foundations. Countless thousands were saved and multitudes miraculously healed. These believers may not have been perfect, but they were alive and on the move: "Day after day, in the temple courts and from house to house, they never stopped teaching and proclaiming the good news that Jesus is the Messiah" (Acts 5:42).

This was the early Church! Could there be anything more exciting?

Even what Old Testament Israel experienced — including Mount Sinai and all the wonders — is almost nothing compared to a genuine New Testament walk with the Lord. "For what was glorious has no glory now in comparison with the surpassing glory. And if what was fading away came with glory, how much greater glory is the glory of that which lasts!" (2 Cor. 3:10-11) *We* are the ones "who with unveiled faces all reflect the Lord's glory, [and] are being transformed into His likeness with ever-increasing glory" (2 Cor. 3:18). *We* are the ones God has lavished His grace on, raising us up with Jesus and seating us with Him in the heavenly realms (Eph. 1:7-8, 2:4-7). *We* are the ones called to be "blameless and pure, children of God without fault in a crooked and depraved generation, in which [we] shine like stars in the universe as [we] hold out the word of life" (Phil. 2:15-16).

When Peter wrote about the reality of our redemption, he was almost overwhelmed:
"Praise be to the God and Father of our Lord Jesus Christ! In His great mercy He has given us new birth into a living hope through the resurrection of Jesus Christ from the dead, and into an inheritance that can never perish, spoil or fade — kept in heaven for you. ... You are a chosen people, a royal priesthood, a holy nation, a people belonging to God, that you may declare the praises of Him who called you out of darkness into His wonderful light.... . *Even angels long to look into these things*" (1 Pet. 1:3-4, 2:9, 1:12).
But do angels long to look into what we now experience? The thought is almost ludicrous. They are probably bored too!

Are we glowing brightly in the Lord? Do the unsaved see the light of our good deeds and praise our Father in heaven? It doesn't take much consideration to come to a simple conclusion: What we are presently experiencing is *not* what the Word of God describes. *It simply is not happening in most of our lives.*

Yes, God is moving and working in this land: Many congregations are growing, people are being saved, the gifts of the Spirit are being manifest, and prayers are being supernaturally answered. *But all this is occurring on an incredibly limited basis,* both in terms of quality as well as quantity. It would be an insult to Jesus to suggest that this is *everything* He died for, that this is the evidence of the outpouring of the Spirit, that this is even a fraction of what God intended. No! There must be something radically more — something of a completely different order, something worthy of the Lord — or the Bible is not true.

Many of us have been on a spiritual odyssey: We have gone from message to message, from church to church, from conference to conference, from teaching to teaching, each time with renewed hope and expectation, each time thinking, "This is it! This is the real thing." And each time we have been sadly disappointed. *The new teaching only took us so far. The new experience only went so deep.* It was, and is, a poor replica of the New Testament faith.

Why do so many believers hear so many sermons, listen to so many teaching tapes, read so many faith-building books, follow so many spiritual formulas, make so many efforts to grow and never seem to change? Is this what life in the Spirit is all about?

Let's be totally honest with ourselves and, for one moment, forget about all the excuses we have heard. When *you* read the New Testament, what do you see? What would you be led to expect? If you sat down and read the gospels and the Book of Acts, closed your Bible, and then pictured what would have happened over those next few centuries, would you have thought that 2,000 years later the world still would not be fully evangelized? Would you have dreamed that *twenty centuries* would come and go without Jesus coming back? And if someone were to tell you that by the year 2000 there would be *hundreds of millions* of "Spirit-filled" believers across the globe, would you ever imagine that the world could be in its present condition? Even my eleven-year-old daughter said to me after reading Acts chapter two, "If we had the same power they had, the whole world would be saved in a matter of months!"

It is true that "multitudes are now turning to Christ in all parts of the world. How unbearably tragic it would be, though, if the millions of Asia, South America and Africa were led to believe that the best we can hope for from the Way of Christ is the level of Christianity visible in Europe and America today, a level that has left us teetering on the edge of world destruction" (Dallas Willard). How will this ever change?

Oswald Chambers, the godly author of the devotional classic *My Utmost for His Highest*, found a way out. But his deliverance came through a crisis that began when he heard there was more to be had in the Lord. And that is where it must start for us. The born again, Spirit-filled life is supposed to be different!

Chambers had come to know the Lord as a boy and, in his own words, "enjoyed the presence of Jesus Christ wonderfully." Yet it was some years before he totally gave himself over to the Lord's service; he did not hear about the baptism of the Holy Spirit until he was a tutor of philosophy in Dunoon College. After listening to F. B. Meyer speak on the Holy Spirit, he went to his room "and asked God simply and definitely for the baptism of the Holy Spirit, whatever that meant.

"From that day on for four years, [he said,] nothing but the overruling grace of God and the kindness of friends kept me out of an asylum. God used me during those years for the conversion of souls, but I had no conscious communion with Him. The Bible was the dullest, most uninteresting book in existence, and the sense of depravity, the vileness and bad-motivedness of my nature was terrific. I see now that God was taking me by the light of the Holy Spirit and His Word through every ramification of my being.

"The last three months of those years things reached a climax. I was getting very desperate. I knew no one who had what I wanted. *IN FACT, I DID NOT KNOW WHAT I WANTED. BUT I KNEW THAT IF WHAT I HAD WAS ALL THE CHRISTIANITY THERE WAS, THE THING WAS A FRAUD.*"

That is the revelation we need. May God open our eyes and help us to see! What we are presently walking in is *not* all it was played up to be. It cannot possibly be the same brand of faith as that which shook the ancient world. If our God "is able to do immeasurably more than all we *ask* or *imagine*" (Eph. 3:20), why do we *ask* for so much (according to His will!) and apparently receive so little? Why do the imaginations and dreams we had when we were first saved just seem like immature fantasies now? We talk about doing the "greater works" of Jesus, but let's be real: Ten of us doing the *same works* of the Lord would challenge all of America overnight. (I wonder if there are even *five* of us who could handle such an anointing — along with all the media exposure — without letting it go to our heads.)

Preachers, can you be candid enough to stand up at your healing services and say, "If what we are seeing is a true reflection of the Lord, then He must be fickle, arbitrary and relatively powerless!" Evangelists, are you willing to boldly proclaim at your "revival" meetings, "If what we are experiencing is the fullness of the Spirit, then we ought to quit right now and go home!" Pastors, will you express clearly to your flocks, "If the quality of life we are manifesting in the Lord is the best there is, then our churches are in trouble!" Believers, do you have the courage to get alone with God and say to Him honestly, "If what I have is all the Christianity there is, then the thing is a fraud!"

God would actually be pleased with us if we did this. *He* was the One who said through His servant Malachi, "Oh, that one of you would shut the temple doors, so that you would not light useless fires on My altar!" (Mal. 1:10) That's right, *useless fires*; and God was the One who said so! He would rather that we close down the show if we won't clean up our acts. Why continue with our rituals if the Lord does not approve?

Wouldn't it be glorious if ministers across the country said to their flocks on Sunday, "We're not having church today! We're not going on with an empty routine! No new programs or plans! We're going to confess our sins to God and acknowledge our spiritual bankruptcy. And we're going to stay here all morning and pray for revival." What would happen to our country if congregations did this just one Sunday each month — without giving up or losing heart? The face of our nation would change.

We need to think of those we've preached to for years — with little sign of lasting victory in their lives — and cry out, "Where is the power of the gospel?" We need to remember all those who died of terrible sickness and disease — never receiving their expected healing — and cry out, "Where is the power of the gospel?" We need to walk the streets of our corrupt cities, looking at the addicts and winos and prostitutes — in spite of churches on almost every street — and cry out, "Where is the power of the gospel?" We need to consider how the Mormons and New Age groups are aggressively infiltrating our communities — while our own feeble witnessing efforts lack convicting authority — and cry out, "Where is the power of the gospel?"

We *must* force a crisis in our lives. More of the same will only produce more of the same. Something fundamental, something basic, must change. Just *building ourselves up* with more faith, more consecration, more soul-winning, more Scripture meditation or more love will never turn the tide. All of these things are good. They are necessary ingredients to our spiritual lives. But they, in and of themselves, cannot deliver us from our present rut.

Our whole orientation to spiritual things must be altered, *and altered from the roots*. We don't need more methods and techniques. No! We need the Lord Himself to come down and lift us up. Nothing else will do. And when we seek Him with all our heart and all our soul, when our very being aches with desire for His visitation, when we are consumed with hunger for His reality, when we radically cut back on other activities in order to seek His face, *then* we are ripe for transformation — *then* the BREAKTHROUGH will come. We can be immersed into the very nature and authority of the Lord. How miserable it is that the "average Christian is so cold and so contented with his wretched condition that there is no vacuum of desire into which the blessed Spirit can rush in satisfying fullness" (A. W. Tozer).

But Oswald Chambers could not be content; the vacuum of desire was too great. He came to the critical juncture:

"Those of you who know the experience, know very well how God brings one to the point of utter despair, and I got to the place where I did not care whether everyone knew how bad I was. I cared for nothing on earth, saving to get out of my present condition."

At the end of a little meeting, after singing "Touch Me Again Lord," Chambers said, "I felt nothing, but I knew emphatically my time had come, and I rose to my feet. I had no vision of God, only a sheer, dogged determination to take God at His Word and to prove this thing for myself. And I stood up and said so.

"That was bad enough, but what followed was ten times worse. After I sat down, the speaker, who knew me well, said, 'That is very good of our brother. He has spoken like that as an example to the rest of you.'

"Up I got again and said, 'I got up for no one's sake. I got up for my own sake. Either Christianity is a downright fraud, or I have not got hold of the right end of the stick.' And then, and there, I claimed the gift of the Holy Spirit in dogged committal on Luke 11:13. I had no vision of Heaven or of angels. I had nothing. I was as dry and empty as ever, no power or realization of God, no witness of the Holy Spirit."

But something supernatural had taken place. God had taken hold of his life. Four years later Chambers said, "If the previous years had been Hell on earth, these four years have truly been Heaven on earth. Glory be to God, the last aching abyss of the human heart is filled to overflowing with the love of God. Love is the beginning, love is the middle, and love is the end. After He comes in, all you see is 'Jesus only, Jesus ever.' "

Looking back, Oswald Chambers could say, "The baptism of the Holy Ghost does not make you think of time or eternity; it is one amazing, glorious now. ... It is no wonder that I talk so much about an altered disposition: God altered mine; I was there when He did it, and I have been there ever since."

Oh, for an encounter with the Lord! The spiritual crisis is worth it all. GOD is at the end of the tunnel.

Are you willing to become consumed to the core of your being with desire for God? Are you willing to let Him strip you of all confidence in the flesh until you get to the point of total dependence on Him? Are you willing — in brokenness and humility — to stand out from the crowd that is apparently satisfied with leftover bread? Are you willing to be emptied and emptied again so that God can fully fill you? The choice is entirely yours.

How far are you willing to go?

Chapter Four

The Spirit Does the Work!

We have little idea of just how dependent we have become on human means. If we don't spend thousands of dollars advertising our special rallies and activities we can hardly draw a crowd. Without extensive mailings, only a handful of people will be interested in our gospel activities and products. In our media-soaked society, we have found it necessary to resort to full-color magazine displays, catchy marketing phrases, massive bumper sticker campaigns, and special celebrity guests at our meetings. And while none of this is necessarily sinful or wrong, it is surely symptomatic of one thing: We don't have revival fire in our midst! The *Holy Spirit* is not drawing the crowds.

Just look at what happens when the Spirit of God is mightily at work.

The year was 1740. Nathan Cole, an unsaved (yet religiously interested) farmer living twelve miles from Middletown, Connecticut, had heard that George Whitefield would soon be preaching in his area. He didn't want to miss the opportunity of hearing Whitefield speak. John Pollock relates the story:

"Shortly before nine in the morning of October 23, 1740, Nathan Cole was working in his fields when a horseman galloped by, calling out that 'Mr. Whitefield is to preach at Middletown.' Cole dropped his tool, ran home to his wife to tell her to get ready, 'then ran to my pasture for my horse with all my might, fearing I would be too late.' " (And the only "advertising" was the single sentence of a single horseman speeding by!)

He put his wife on the horse with him "and pressed forward as fast as the horse could manage. Whenever it laboured too hard he jumped off, eased his wife into the saddle and told her not to stop or slack for him while he ran beside her. He would run until too out of breath, then mount again. They rode as if 'fleeing for our lives, all the while fearing we should be too late to hear the sermon.' " (Remember, there were no famous music groups, no special youth activities, not even any miracles of healing or exciting prophecies; only the anointing of God on the message.)

"The fields were deserted; every man and woman must be gone to Middletown. When the Coles reached the high ground overlooking the road which runs from Hartford and Stepney they saw it covered with what looked like a fog. At first Cole thought that it was morning mist drifting from the broad Connecticut River, but as they drew nearer they heard a rumble like thunder and soon found that the cloud was of dust made by horses cantering down the road.

"Cole slipped his horse into a vacant space and when Mrs. Cole looked at the dust-coated riders, their hats and clothes all of a colour with their horses, she cried, 'Law, our clothes will all be spoiled, see how they look!'

"On they rode, no one speaking a word [for three miles!], 'but everyone pressing forward in great haste,' until the cavalcade cantered into Middletown and Cole saw the space in front of the old meeting-house on the edge of the town jammed with bodies. The Coles were in time: the ministers, a phalanx of black, were moving across to the hastily erected scaffold platform where Whitefield would preach. As Cole dismounted and shook off the dust, 'I looked towards the river and saw the ferry boats running swift backward and forward bringing over loads of people, and the oars rowed nimble and quick. Everything, men, horses and boats seemed to be struggling for life. The land and banks over the river looked black with people and horses.'

"Whitefield came forward on the platform. He looks almost angelical, thought Cole: 'a young, slim, slender youth before some thousands of people with a bold, un-daunted countenance. And my hearing how God was with him everywhere as he came along, it solemnized my mind and put me into a trembling fear before he began to preach, for he looked as if he was clothed with authority from the Great God' ... and my hearing him preach gave me a heart wound and by God's blessing my old foundation was broken up and I saw my righteousness would not save me."

The divine arrows so penetrated Cole's heart, that although he had previously believed that he could be saved by his own good works, an intense conviction of sin came upon him *and lasted for two years,* after which time he was wonderfully born from above. Nowadays, we are lucky to get the people to respond to a high-pressure, on the spot invitation. *But the Word on fire burns deep.*

And how did the twenty-five year old Whitefield describe this event in his journal? "Preached to about four thousand people at eleven o'clock, and again, in the afternoon at Wallingford, fourteen miles from Middletown." That was it! Nothing special or out of the ordinary; just another day of ministry — preached in the morning and preached in the afternoon. Today we'd be boasting about it for months to come: "Wow! What an awesome meeting!" Actually, the only thing in Whitefield's journal entry for that day that drew special mention was this: He was impressed with the simplicity of his host "and the order wherewith his children conducted their family devotions"!

The ministry of John Wesley also drew the crowds. Wesley lacked Whitefield's dramatic flair — one listener, after hearing him preach said, "But for an occasional lifting of his right hand, he might have been a speaking statue" — and in the natural, he much preferred studying in a quiet room to preaching outdoors to the multitudes. But he was compelled by compassion to reach out to the lost, and the lost were not in the churches. (They're not in the churches today either!)

On Friday, May 28, 1742, Wesley, along with a friend named John Taylor, arrived on the outskirts of Newcastle-upon-Tyne in England. Wesley was amazed at the sinfulness of the people, right down to the little children, and saw at once that it was a ripe place for the gospel. The next morning *at seven o'clock*, Wesley went down to what he described as "the poorest and most contemptible part of the town." Then, standing at the end of the street, he and Taylor began to sing Psalm 100. First three or four people came to see what was happening; soon there were three or four hundred watching and listening with curiosity.

"Then Wesley gave a message on Isaiah 53:5, and before he had finished the crowd had grown to almost *fifteen hundred*. The people still stood there after he had closed the service, gaping and staring in their astonishment at such an unusual sight. Wesley, in his matter-of-fact way, made the briefest of announcements. 'If you desire to know who I am, my name is John Wesley. At five in the evening, with God's help, I design to preach here again.' And with that he left them." That was his publicity! He came into the town unadvertised, preached at 7:00 A.M., and said he would be back at 5:00 P.M. How incredibly simple! And remember who his audience was: *people who previously had little or no interest in God.*

"In the evening the numbers had swelled to incredible proportions. In Moorfields and on Kennington Commons [where he had previously preached] Wesley had faced congregations of up to twenty thousand, *but this was more than he had ever seen.* Afterwards, the poor people were ready to tread him underfoot 'out of pure love and kindness.' It was some time before he could get away" (A. Skevington Wood).

W. H Fitchett wrote:
"For the gathering of these crowds Wesley employed none of the familiar modern devices. There were no advertisements, no local committees, no friendly newspapers, no attractions of great choirs. It is a puzzle still to know how the crowds were induced to assemble, for Wesley gives no hints of any organization employed [although he did organize societies for the discipling of the new converts]. *His hearers seemed to wait for him, to spring up before him as if at the signal of some mysterious whisper coming out of space.*"

The Holy Spirit was wooing the people. Revival was in the air.

Now it must be stated clearly: There is nothing wrong with local organizing committees, talented gospel singers, and newspaper and television advertising. But our *reliance* on all these means to bring in the people reveals a sad condition: The Spirit is hardly present and we are trying to make up for His relative absence. To be perfectly frank, we *need* to do all these things right now. Otherwise hardly anyone would show up!

But, if the people in your neighborhood were literally starving and your family alone had food, you wouldn't need to publicize it. Word would get out — like it or not — and your big problem would be how to keep the mobs away. Or if you developed a pill that was a surefire cure for cancer, do you think that you would have to hire an advertising agent? Would a price of five hundred dollars per pill even slow the sales down? Your only concern would be how to manufacture enough!

Then why aren't the crowds knocking down our doors for the bread of life? (It may be happening in other parts of the world, but it is certainly not the norm in the United States.) Why aren't they flocking to us for the only real antidote? It's because we don't have the goods! On top of that, we haven't convinced the world that it is sick, starving and on the verge of eternal death.

In 1905, during the height of the Welsh revival, an eyewitness described a meeting in Liverpool:

"The crowds were pressing against the chapel doors, trying to push their way in, and elderly ladies were climbing over the railings to get to the door, and falling on the

others, were being thrown inside by the police like sacks of flour" (E. Morgan Humphreys).
Jesus was being lifted up, and He was drawing all men to Himself.

Several years later, in 1912, the *Life of Faith* periodical gave an account of the effects of the mighty healing ministry of Stephen Jeffreys:

"Although day after day it has poured in torrents, people have walked miles over the hills to hear the preaching and all over Wales congregations are praying that the revival will spread. ... I sat last night in his packed iron church and saw folk, their faces lit with ecstasy, swaying with emotion, 'The Spirit has come!' shouted one woman, sinking on her knees and bursting into prayer, and fervent ejaculations of contrition and devotion came from all around us as preaching in Welsh, Mr. Jeffreys exhorted his hearers to repent [this was no 'ear-tickling' message!]. For hours it went on and so it will go day after day and night after night. Remarkable cases of healing are reported."

Others have described how in the days of Stephen and George Jeffreys, men would walk down the streets at the close of the service, carrying chairs on their backs. Then they would put the chairs around the meeting hall and sleep there all night! Their wives, coming and relieving them in the morning so they could go to work, would sit in the chairs until three P.M. when the afternoon meeting began. They did all this just to be sure of getting a seat! The miracles and the messages did their own promoting, and everyone came crowding in.

But we have not just leaned on our own efforts to bring *in the people.* We are greatly dependent on our skills to *change the people's lives.* We are coached on exactly how to get our point across (and remember always to look straight into the camera!); we attend seminars on how to succeed in ministry, adopting high-powered business techniques to advance the kingdom of God; and, of course, we can't forget to wear the right clothes! Some have even said, "If you're a good salesman then you'll make a good soul winner" — as if converting a sinner were like closing a sale! And while the Lord is not exalted through sloppiness, carelessness and disorganization, He can work through our weakness and simplicity. We don't need the glamor and the sparkle, we need the glory and the Spirit!

D. Martyn Lloyd Jones tells us about the ministry of "the saintly Robert Murray McCheyne in his church in Dundee [Scotland] in the late 1830's and early 1840's. It has been authenticated so many, many times, that Robert Murray McCheyne had simply to enter the pulpit and before he had opened his mouth people used to begin to weep and were convicted of sin. He had not uttered a word. Why? Well, the explanation was that this man had come from the presence of God and the Spirit was poured forth." Why can't this happen in our meetings? Despite all our efforts, so few are deeply affected. Yet McCheyne didn't even speak and people were being dealt with by God.

Moses told the Lord that if He would not go with the people, then they would not move.

"How will anyone know that You are pleased with me and with Your people unless You go with us? *What else will distinguish me and Your people from all the other people on the face of the earth?*" (Ex. 33:16)
The presence of God makes the difference. Even sinners will recognize it, falling down in our midst and exclaiming, *"God is really among you!"* (1 Cor. 14:24-25) It is the Spirit who convicts.

That is why Paul did not depend on "eloquence or superior wisdom." Rather, he said,

"I resolved to know nothing while I was with you except Jesus Christ and Him crucified. I came to you in weakness and fear, and with much trembling. My message and my preaching were not with wise and persuasive words, but with a demonstration of the Spirit's power, *so that your faith might not rest on men's wisdom, but on God's power*" (1 Cor. 2:1-5).

To the Thessalonians he wrote that "our gospel came to you not simply with words, but also with power, with the Holy Spirit and with deep conviction" (1 Thess. 1:5). This had been the hallmark of the ministry of Jesus: He taught with authority. And now by the Spirit, it is to continue through us.

We are different than all the other religions and cults. They must rely on their own efforts to gain new adherents to their faith. They must be able to convince, persuade and win people over by entirely human means. But we are dependent on the ministry of the Holy Spirit working through our efforts. We in ourselves cannot save a soul. And while we must witness, evangelize, reach out and actively share the Good News with the lost, it is only the Spirit who can save, transform and regenerate. Only He can make a child of hell into a child of heaven. Only He can change sinners into saints. Our goal is not to enlist people in our cause. Our goal is to usher people into the kingdom by the power of the living Word.

Martyn Lloyd Jones recounts the story of a Scottish minister named John Livingstone. Although he was known as a solid preacher, nothing remarkable happened under his ministry until he preached at a special meeting on Monday, June 21, 1630. The devil had tried to discourage Livingstone from delivering the word that day, telling him that he could not speak to such a large crowd. But he overcame the attack and went on to preach on Ezekiel 36:25-26, the work of the Holy Spirit.

After speaking for an hour and a half, "he came to his application, which he had intended to be brief. An hour and a half of exposition outlining the doctrine, then application. But he suddenly found that there was something happening to him, and the application which he had intended to be brief went on for another hour; and as it went on, astounding things were happening. People were falling to the ground, others were breaking down weeping.

"The end of the story was that it was estimated that at least five hundred people were converted as the result of that one sermon. When I say converted, I do not mean that they just came forward at the end. They did not do things like that in those days, there was no need. I do not mean that they signed some form. No, they were converted in the sense that their whole lives changed and they joined the Christian church with no pressure to decision brought upon them, none of the usual machinery that we have become so accustomed to — nothing like that at all. All that only began about the middle of the last century. But this was the power of the Spirit!"

Think of it: no fleshly altar calls, no high-pressure appeals, no invitations with "every head bowed and every eye closed" (as if giving your life to Jesus was a shameful thing that needed to be done in secret), no mechanical reciting of "sinner's prayers." No! Just the long-lasting, heart-changing, captive-freeing power of the gospel! Yet because our preaching lacks punch, because we have not opened the eyes of the sinner to his lost state, because we hardly confront him with the reality of the living God, we have to lean on human techniques as well as a watered-down message. "You don't have to *do* anything," we say. "Simply pray this little prayer — and whether you feel the witness in your heart or not, whether your life changes or not, whether you ever repent of your sin or not — it's done! Isn't that easy?"

All this smacks entirely of human effort; there is little for the Spirit of God to do. But until 150 years ago, things were much different. When John Wesley would preach to the crowds at night, he would press home his appeal and urge the listeners to repent and believe. Then he would leave. If they showed up again at the *five A.M.* meeting, then he would acknowledge that they might, in fact, be serious. If they followed through and joined one of his Methodist societies, giving clear evidence of a changed life, then he knew they were saved! Even though he firmly believed in instantaneous conversion, it was very rare that he would allow people to give immediate testimony of their salvation experience. He wanted to test it out.

But have we learned the lesson? It is one thing to say, "There were 220 *professions* of faith last night. Let's pray that they will prove sincere." It's another thing entirely to say, "What a meeting! Two hundred and twenty people were *saved* last night." Saved according to who? After Peter's first Spirit-baptized sermon, the Word says: "Those who accepted his message [and Peter didn't pull any punches either!] were baptized, and about three thousand *were added to their number that day*" (Acts 2:41). They were saved — and that meant they stayed. *They were also serious*: "They devoted themselves to the apostles' teaching and to the fellowship, to the breaking of bread and to prayer" (Acts 2:42).

But what do we have today when, according to statistics, 80% of those "converted" at our evangelistic campaigns backslide? The plain truth is that we must exchange our modern-day version of the gospel for the real biblical brand. And we must fast and pray earnestly that the Spirit would do the work.

We can't improve on that.

Chapter Five

Has the Gift of Healing Hit a Brick Wall?

God is the Healer of His people! That is a fundamental truth of the Word. Three times in the Law, God repeated this fact:

> "If you listen carefully to the voice of the Lord your God and do what is right in His eyes, if you pay attention to His commands and keep all His decrees, I will not bring on you any of the diseases I brought on the Egyptians, *for I am the Lord, who heals you*" (Ex. 15:26).

> "Worship the Lord your God, and His blessing will be on your food and water. *I will take sickness from among you*, and none will miscarry or be barren in your land. I will give you a full life span" (Ex. 23:25-26).

> "If you pay attention to these laws and are careful to follow them, then the Lord your God will keep His covenant of love with you, as He swore to your forefathers. ... *The Lord will keep you free from every disease.* He will not inflict on you the horrible diseases you knew in Egypt, but He will inflict them on all who hate you" (Deut. 7:12,15).

That's why David could proclaim: "Praise the Lord, O my soul, and forget not all His benefits — who forgives all your sins *and heals all your diseases*" (Ps. 103:2-3). That's why the psalmist could promise: "If you make the Most High your dwelling — even the Lord, who is my refuge — *then no harm will befall you, no disaster will come near your tent* (Ps. 91:9-10).

According to the Book of Proverbs, words of godly wisdom "are life to those who find them *and health to a man's whole body*" (Prov. 4:22). Fearing the Lord in humility and turning away from evil *"will bring health to your body and nourishment to your bones"* (Prov. 3:7-8). Reckless words may "pierce like a sword, *but the tongue of the wise brings healing*" (Prov. 12:18). This is the heart of the message of Proverbs: Godliness leads to life; wickedness leads to death.

As for the prophets, their entire burden for Israel and the nations can be summed up in one word: restoration. (This is actually the original meaning of the Hebrew word for healing: "making whole, restoring.") Just as Israel was *smitten* by the Lord — and this meant judgment on their land, their economy, their families and their bodies — so the Lord would heal His repentant people. This translated out to complete reversal of all judgment. If the "smiting" was real, then the "healing" was just as real. God would fully restore.

"*I will heal My people* and will let them enjoy abundant peace and security." What did this actually mean?

"I will bring Judah and Israel back from captivity and will rebuild them as they were before. I will cleanse them from all the sin they have committed against Me and will forgive all their sins of rebellion against Me. Then this city will bring Me renown, joy, praise and honor before all the nations on earth that hear of all the good things I do for it;

and they will be in awe and will tremble at the abundant prosperity and peace I provide for it" (Jer. 33:6-9). Hallelujah! And there would be no sickness there: "No one living in Zion will say, 'I am ill'; [for] the sins of those who dwell there will be forgiven" (Is. 33:24).

And all this was under the Old Covenant. Now we have a *better* covenant founded on *better* promises (Heb. 8:6). So, if sickness was an Old Covenant *curse* and healing was an Old Covenant *blessing*, is it possible that under the newer (and better!) covenant sickness has become a *blessing* and healing a *curse*? Of course not! Under the Old Covenant, God inflicted sickness on those who *hated* Him. Under the New Covenant does He now inflict it on those who *love* Him? Of course not!

This is not to say that everyone who is sick is guilty of some specific sin or is under the judgment of God, nor is it to say that God cannot teach us something through sickness, even though sickness is not a blessing from above. And there *are* spiritual people who are infirm. Our job is not to judge or minister condemnation; our job is to minister healing.

Of course I recognize that there are believers whose lives have been cut short as martyrs for the faith, while others suffer greatly in prison because they will not deny the Lord. God never promised to deliver us from persecution. He did promise to deliver us from sickness.

The Scriptures are perfectly clear: *Nowhere in the Bible is sickness, in and of itself, ever referred to as a blessing.* Contrary to the opinion expressed recently by C. Everett Koop, our country's former Surgeon General and a man rightly respected as a national Christian leader, sickness is not often "the *proof* of God's special favor." Healing is!

As we read through the pages of the newer and better covenant, the picture gets even clearer. Here are some typical passages from the gospels:

> "When evening came, many who were demon-possessed were brought to [Jesus], and He drove out the spirits with a word *and healed all the sick*" (Matt. 8:16).
>
> "Jesus went throughout all the towns and villages, teaching in their synagogues, preaching the good news of the kingdom *and healing every disease and sickness*" (Matt. 9:35).
>
> "When Jesus landed and saw a large crowd, *He had compassion on them and healed their sick*" (Matt. 14:14).
>
> "People brought all their sick to Him and begged Him to let the sick just touch the edge of His cloak, *and all who touched Him were healed*" (Matt. 14:35-36).
>
> "Great crowds came to Him, bringing the lame, the blind, the crippled, the mute and many others, and laid them at His feet; *and He healed them*. The people were amazed when they saw the mute speaking, the crippled made well, the lame walking and the blind seeing. *And they praised the God of Israel*" (Matt. 15:30-31).

He was still the same God, except things were much better now! This was the beginning of the New Covenant.

And why did Jesus do what He did? Why did He *never* refuse to heal anyone? This was His own explanation:

> "I tell you the truth, the Son can do nothing by Himself; He can only do what He sees His Father doing, because whatever the Father does the Son also does. ... Do not believe Me unless I do what My Father does. ... Anyone who has seen Me has seen the Father. ... Believe Me when I say that I am in the Father and the Father is in Me; or at

least believe on the evidence of the miracles themselves"
(John 5:19, 10:37, 14:9,11).

Could anything be more plain? Jesus healed the sick because that was His Father's will! God's promises had not
changed. In fact, when Jesus healed the sick He was manifesting the very nature of God to us: "The Lord is good to all; He
has *compassion* on all He has made" (Ps. 145:9). Jesus showed
us what His Father was really like.

And nothing changed in the Book of Acts. In fact, the
crowds knew that Jesus had indeed risen from the dead and
sent down His Spirit because His disciples were doing the
very same works that He had done.

"Everyone was filled with awe, and *many wonders and
miraculous signs* were done by the apostles" (Acts 2:43).

"People brought the sick into the streets and laid them
on beds and mats so that at least Peter's shadow might fall
on them as he passed by. Crowds gathered also from the
towns around Jerusalem, bringing their sick and those tor-
mented by evil spirits, *and all of them were healed*" (Acts
5:15-16).

"Now Stephen, a man full of God's grace and power,
did *great wonders and miraculous signs* among the
people" (Acts 6:8).

"When the crowds heard Philip and saw *the miraculous
signs* he did, they all paid close attention to what he said.
With shrieks, evil spirits came out of many, *and many
paralytics and cripples were healed*" (Acts 8:6-7).

"[Publius'] father was sick in bed, suffering from fever
and dysentery. Paul went in to see him and, after prayer,
placed his hands on him *and healed him*. When this had
happened, *the rest of the sick on the island came and were
cured*" (Acts 28:8-9).

What an awesome account! And these are only a few short excerpts.

But the story does not end here. *Gifts of healing and miraculous powers* were deposited within the Church for good (1 Cor. 12-14). There is not a stitch of evidence that these manifestations of the Spirit were ever to depart in this age. Absolutely not! God certainly has not changed. His *newer* and *better* covenant has not changed. *And the needs of mankind have not changed.*

It's pathetic to hear people argue: "Divine healing is not for today. All these supernatural manifestations in our day come from another spiritual force." This would mean, that while in the gospels it was the devil who often made people sick and God who made them well (Matt. 12:22; Luke 13:10-16; Acts 10:38), today it is God who makes them sick and the devil who makes them well! How absurd! Can anyone picture the Lord coming to the bed of a sick little girl with her parents praying by her side, "Touch her Lord," laying His hand on her and making her *sicker*? The thought is revolting.

Some would say: "That's fine and good for Bible days. Maybe Jesus healed back then. But didn't the gifts of the Spirit cease to operate after the first few centuries?" Yes, by and large, they did. The Church lost much of her early inheritance, including justification by faith and the priesthood of every believer. But, just as these truths began to be restored to the body 500 years ago, in the last 100 years, the gifts of the Spirit have begun to be restored. *We are on the way back to the foundations of our faith.* And the best is yet to come! According to Jonathan Edwards, who was anything but an excitable Charismatic:

"... we have reason from Scripture prophecy to suppose, that at the commencement of that last great outpouring of the Spirit of God, that is to be in the latter ages of the world, the manner of the work will be very extraordinary, and such as never yet been seen ... It may be reasonably expected that the extraordinary manner of the work then will bear some proportion to the very extraordinary events, and that glorious change in the state of the world, which God will bring to pass by it."

Of course, there are those who expect a worldwide, end-time revival who still have problems with divine healing. "It's not so simple," they say. "What about Paul's thorn?" Well, what about it? Read Second Corinthians chapters 11 and 12 a dozen times over and see if Paul ever mentions sickness there at all. Scholars are *still* debating about the exact nature of his "thorn in the flesh." And it is erroneous to compare our problems with Paul's thorn in the flesh. Paul's thorn was given to him "to keep [him] from being conceited because of [his] surpassingly great revelations" (2 Cor. 12:7). We flatter ourselves far too much when we see the diseases or tragedies that come our way as thorns God has given us to keep *us* humble.

"But did Paul see everyone healed? Didn't Paul tell Timothy to *drink a little wine* for his stomach problems?" (1 Tim. 5:23) Absolutely! Paul wanted to see him well, not sick (wine was widely used in those days for medicinal purposes). "Then why didn't *God* heal Timothy?" We simply don't know; the Scriptures do not say. But this much is sure: If *God* wanted Timothy to be sick, Paul had no business advising him to try to get better! If sickness is a blessing from God, then why go to doctors? Why not simply say, "Father, Your will be done," and remain sick?

No, God is *for* healing, not against it; He is *for* good medical care, not opposed to it. In fact, if it is *the Lord* who makes people *sick*, "then would not every physician be a law-breaker, every trained nurse be defying the Almighty, every hospital [be] a house of rebellion instead of a house of mercy, and instead of supporting hospitals should we not then do our utmost to close them?" (F. F. Bosworth) If God were the primary force behind sickness, then the entire medical profession would be in direct contradiction to His work! I know that some teachers claim that "God still heals, but *only* through medical and natural means." Yet this position is really bizarre. It would mean that, whereas in the Bible Jesus healed primarily the incurable (the ones doctors and nature could *not* help), today He only heals the curable (the ones doctors and nature *can* help). Not only so, it would also imply that an atheist with a good doctor experiences more of God's healing power than a faithful child of God who has no medical care!

"But wait one second. Didn't Paul leave Trophimus sick at Miletus?" Yes, and we don't know why Trophimus wasn't healed (2 Tim. 4:20). Maybe he didn't believe he would be healed; maybe he had not taken care of his body and he needed to simply rest and recover; maybe he was in the process of getting well; maybe Paul prayed and nothing happened this particular time. *We don't always receive everything God has graciously provided for us.* But to base your theology of healing on this isolated, unexplained instance is really grasping at straws.

The overwhelming testimony of the Word of God is abundantly clear: God's ideal will for His obedient children is healing. That is the doctrine expressed in hundreds of verses. There really is no room to doubt. In fact, it was *because* the sick were so regularly healed in New Testament times that cases like that of Trophimus stand out.

John G. Lake, a man who personally witnessed tens of thousands of genuine miracles, has given us wise counsel:

"We may never get one half or one quarter of the way toward the ideal. But never try to degrade God's purpose and bring it down to your level. But by the grace of God put the standard up there where Jesus put it, and then get as near it as you can."

Don't make the Word fit your experience, make your experience fit the Word!

Listen to the instruction of James:

"Is any one of you in trouble? He should pray. [This certainly has not changed.] Is anyone happy? Let him sing songs of praise. [This hasn't changed either.] *Is any one of you sick?* He should call the elders of the church to pray over him and anoint him with oil in the name of the Lord. *And the prayer offered in faith* [not the oil], *will make the sick person well; the Lord will raise him up.* [And *this* hasn't changed! When we truly pray in faith we see the same results.] If he has sinned, he will be forgiven" (James 5:13-15).

Even if this Scripture is not mainly for believers suffering with colds and sore throats, it certainly applies to those who are seriously ill. Miraculous healing is supposed to happen. It was the hallmark of the early Church for decades *after* the apostles died.

Based on the clear evidence of the Scriptures, there are two crucial lessons that must be learned:

1) If anyone says that the Old Covenant promises of healing do not apply to believers today, or that the miraculous pattern of the gospels, Acts, and the epistles is not to be the pattern of the Church today, then *they are wrong.*

2) If anyone says that the healings and miracles presently occurring in "Spirit-filled" meetings in the United States today are anything close to complete restoration of New Testament power, then *they are wrong*. (It doesn't matter if skeptical theologians and teachers try to tell us that our limited success in praying for the sick is proof that healing is not for today. Our position is unshakeable: Even if no one was healed, the testimony of the Word is too clear to deny; and, we've seen God do too much in our lives to ever question that He is still the same healing Lord. There are countless documented healings in answer to believing prayer.)

It seems so obvious: God still wants to heal and deliver His people, but in most cases, chronic conditions persist, terminal diseases are not cured, the blind are still blind, and the crippled are still crippled. *God simply is not doing most of what He promised to do.* Something must be wrong!

But don't just take my word for it; attend some American "miracle services" for yourself. Here is what you will see: *A small percentage* of the sick are definitely healed (praise God for that), while almost all of the really tragic cases — like miserably twisted quadriplegics or those in the last stages of wasting disease — are completely unchanged. Maybe one or two will get out of their wheelchairs, or someone who was legally blind will be able to see (and praise God for that too), but nothing that can compare with the general New Testament pattern ever happens here. And then, so many lose their healings, while others are only partially healed.

Of course, we know all the reasons why the sick are *not* healed: They were ignorant of the promises of God; they failed to confess their healing; they needed to grow up and pray for healing on their own, rather than have someone else pray for them; they were in unbelief; the whole congregation was in unbelief; they were trusting in the healing evangelist instead of in the Lord; more prayer and fasting were needed; the anointing had lifted; it was a demon and not actually a sickness; they had to forgive someone or make restitution; they really needed inner-healing first; or there was a curse put on one of their ancestors ...

But didn't all these things exist in the days of the Lord's earthly ministry? Yet *He* healed all who came to Him in faith. And didn't these same obstacles exist in the days of the apostles? Yet *they* were able to get radically greater results than we do. And don't these very difficulties persist in the rest of the world today? Yet many contemporary believers have seen God do extraordinary miracles in nations other than the United States. They have seen the dead raised on numerous occasions and witnessed hands grow out of little fleshy stumps and eyeballs appear in empty sockets. Yet when they minister in America, they are frustrated with the lack of similar results.

This is exactly how far we have fallen from New Testament authority and power: Today we interpret our services for the deaf (and it is a good thing that we do); *Jesus healed them.*

Then why are we going on as if everything is great and the Spirit is being mightily poured out? Because we're sleepwalking! We're not being totally open. We're afraid to say, "Wait one minute. We're *supposed* to see these cripples leaping for joy. We're *supposed* to see these mutes praising God out loud. We're *supposed* to see these cancer victims made whole by the hundreds. *It's not supposed to be so hard to be healed.*" We're afraid to speak like that because people might say, "You're quenching the Spirit! You're hindering people's faith."

But for years we've remained silent — and the healings have hardly flowed. For years we've said, "Only believe" — and the results are still tragically disappointing. How the heart of God must hurt for these suffering people! And how He must long to manifest His full power and glory.

First we believed that the answer was to be found in the Pentecostal outpouring; then we put our expectation in the Charismatic renewal; after that we discovered the Word of Faith message; now we're excited about a whole new spiritual flow. Yet, as much as God has done through each of these movements, we still find ourselves encountering so many terribly sick people — in our churches, our families and our communities — and so few of them are being made whole through us.

Maybe if we *speak up* something will change. Maybe the Lord won't show us the *greater* hindrances to healing in our day until we begin to say, "Thank God for everything He *is* doing — for every healing, every deliverance, every prophecy and every word of knowledge. Let's continue to pray and believe, but let's publicly admit that the awesome miracles, the genuine signs and wonders, the acts of God that could shake a whole city, are not being performed in our midst." Maybe when we begin to lift our voices at our prayer meetings and cry out, "Lord, we're ashamed. Lord, our hearts are breaking. Lord, show us the way!" — maybe then God will move.

Right now, we have come to the end of our rope.

Chapter Six

How Painful Are Honest Words!

God is not impressed with hype. He has no place for exaggerations. Big speeches do not influence Him. Sensational claims do not fool Him. He only cares for truth. And while we can easily deceive others (and ourselves), we will *never* deceive the Lord. His "eyes are like blazing fire"; He has "the sharp doubled-edged sword"; He is "the faithful and true Witness" (Rev. 2:18,12, 3:14). He never says, "I think." He only says, "I know." To each of the churches addressed in the Book of Revelation, His words were always the same: *"I know ... "*

The believers in Sardis had a name. They were big shots in the kingdom. But Jesus wasn't moved: "*I know* your deeds; you have a reputation of being alive, but you are dead" (Rev. 3:1). What other people thought was completely wrong.

The Laodiceans looked so good on the outside. They seemed to have it all together. They were the church that had arrived — the most prosperous, the most blessed, the most anointed (they probably boasted that they had the "fastest

growing congregations" in Asia Minor). But Jesus saw past
the glitter and sparkle:

> "*I know* your deeds. ... You say, 'I am rich; I have ac-
> quired wealth and do not need a thing.' But you do not
> realize that you are wretched, pitiful, poor, blind and
> naked" (Rev. 3:15, 17).

The Lord's words stripped off the veneer. He sees. He speaks.
He knows.

What would Jesus say to us today? If He appeared on
nationwide Christian TV, what would His message be? How
much of what we have today is reputation, and how much is
reality? Are we a militant Church or a mutant Church? Jesus
says, "*I know* ..." Are we willing to hear *the truth*?

> "We are only what we are in the dark; all the rest is
> reputation. What God looks at is what we are in the dark
> — the imaginations of our minds, the thoughts of our
> heart, the habits of our bodies; these are the things that
> mark us in God's sight. ... Character is what you are in the
> dark" (Oswald Chambers).

What is the character of the contemporary Church? How do
we rate in the dark?

> Remember: God sees *where* no man sees; God sees *what*
> no one man sees; God sees *when* no one man sees.
> Everywhere ... everything ... always.

> "If I say, 'Surely the darkness will hide me and the
> light become night around me,' even the darkness will not
> be dark to You; the night will shine like the day, for dark-
> ness is as light to You" (Ps. 139:11-12).

His searching rays expose and disclose. Let us run to the light
that we may see. *We have already been seen.*

We say, "We are so rich! Our gospel goods are being exported across the globe, our victory videos will soon be seen in every nation, and our miracle ministries are poised to reach the whole world. Devil, look out! The American Church is here." But Jesus says, "*I know ...* " How pathetic our boasting must seem.

What was the greatest weakness of the church of Sardis? "*You have a reputation* of being alive ..." They believed what they heard about themselves! What was the greatest fault of the Laodicean church? "*You do not realize* that you are wretched, pitiful, poor, blind and naked ..." They thought they were so well off! It is bad enough to be in a wretched, pitiful, poor, blind and naked state. But not to realize it — *that* is the real tragedy!

We do not realize our true condition either. We too have a great reputation. But Jesus knows the truth. What will it take to open our eyes? Consider these honest words. They may be painful, but they are right.

"Many of our churches are worshiping an absentee God" (Leonard Ravenhill). There has been so much disobedience and defilement, so much carnality and corruption, that we have greatly driven the presence of God away. It is possible for believers to continue praying, having family devotions, witnessing, singing choruses, tithing, and attending services, *and not even know that the Spirit of the Lord has become distant.* We have become so accustomed to the superficial that we hardly miss the supernatural. We are more Spirit-frilled than Spirit-filled. We are so used to the "outer fringe of His works" (Job 26:14) that we often forget the inner essence of His ways.

Where is the glory? Where is the sense of awe? Where is
God's majesty? How often does His voice resound in our
midst — His shattering, shaking voice? How often do His
signs and wonders cause us to cry out, "It is the Lord!" How
often are we left speechless — staggered, stunned and silent
— because of the great things He has done? *Where is the
presence of God?*

What a shame! We believe in our exaggerated reports.
We have been duped by our fabulous words. Dozens of ministries throughout the land claim to have either outstanding,
overwhelming or sensational signs, wonders and miracles.
They commonly report spectacular acts of God. To hear
them talk, you would almost think that compared to them,
the apostles were spiritual novices. (Don't laugh. Some
teachers claim that if Paul had had *our* revelation, he
wouldn't have had his thorn in the flesh; and if Stephen had
known his full authority, he wouldn't have been martyred.
Rather than laugh, we should weep.) Maybe the apostles
will admire the contemporary saints one day — but that day
is certainly not today.

Our American "signs, wonders and miracles" are hardly
worthy of the name. How clearly are they *signs* — definite
indications that almighty God is at work? In what sense are
they *wonders* if they don't cause astonishment and amaze-
ment? How can we call them *miracles* when the Greek word
literally means "mighty deeds"? How many *mighty* manifestations do we witness today?

The fact is, we are far from true *apostolic* authority in this
country, even though we love to use the term. Actually, it
seems that being apostolic is the "in thing" these days, especially for pastors who have started more than one church. But
let's not forget Paul's words: "The things that mark an apostle

[are] signs, wonders and miracles" (2 Cor. 12:12). And he meant the real thing.

Do we want God's glory restored? Are we ready for end-time power? Then let's face up to honest words, however painful they may be.

Paris Reidhead, who has served as an inner-city pastor, a missionary to Sudan and a Third World economic adviser, recently wrote:
> "During more than forty years spent in service to the Lord I have come to realize that the mass-produced product now passing for 'Christian' bears little or no resemblance to the powerful reality of Christ that can and must be the hallmark of every true child of God."

Evangelical leader Carl Henry has commented that, "we little sense how much of what we possess of a practical Christianity really is an apostate compromise with the spirit of this age."

J. Edwin Orr, the noted revival scholar and speaker, wrote shortly before his death:
> "Defective evangelism has become a national scandal. While evangelistic enterprises are claiming untold numbers of converts, a national poll announcing that multimillions claim to be 'born-again,' yet a national newspaper notes that the 'so-called evangelical awakening' seems to have had no effect upon the morals of the nation, while murder, robbery, rape, prostitution, pornography and the other social evils are abounding."

There are well-meaning preachers in America today who say, "Don't pray for revival. Revival is already here!" But do they really know what they are saying? Richard Owen

Roberts has given us an incredible description of what true revival, ideally speaking, is about:

"Consider every church in your community with every church member marching together in perfect harmony — every individual sharing precisely with every other individual the heartbeat of Jesus Christ. Imagine not one sleeping Christian left, not one backslidden believer remaining, but all alike devout and intent on seeing the will of Jesus Christ accomplished. To this startling picture add the same power of the Holy Spirit that transformed bumbling Peter into a Pentecost preacher. Unleash all this transforming power against the forces of sin and evil in your community. That is what revival is."

How can anyone call what we are presently experiencing *revival?* Yet we are not only in desperate need of revival, we are in need of resurrection and redirection. *Many of us are more dead than alive, more off than on, more wrong than right.* Are we contending for the very same faith "that was once for all entrusted to the saints" (Jude 3)?

Over thirty years ago, A. W. Tozer could say,

"The American genius for getting things done quickly and easily with little concern for quality or permanence has bred a virus that has infected the whole evangelical Church in the United States and, through our literature, our evangelists and our missionaries, has spread all over the world. ... Instant Christianity is twentieth-century orthodoxy. I wonder whether the man who wrote Philippians 3:7-16 would recognize it as the faith for which he finally died. I am afraid he would not."

What would Tozer say if he were alive today? Worse yet, what would Paul say?

Would Paul look at our modern innovations, our advanced techniques and latest revelations and say, "I have no praise for you, for your meetings do more harm than good" (1 Cor. 11:17)? Would he see how far our gospel preaching has departed from the cross and ask, "Who has bewitched you? Before your very eyes Jesus Christ was clearly portrayed as crucified" (Gal. 3:1)? Would he find among us what he feared he would find among the Corinthians: "quarreling, jealousy, outbursts of anger, factions, slander, gossip, arrogance and disorder" (2 Cor. 12:20)? (This actually sounds like some of our congregational business meetings or denominational conventions.)

Because of divisions among the *city-wide* Corinthian church, Paul could not address them as spiritual, but as carnal — not as mature, but as mere infants in Christ. "You are still worldly. For since there is jealousy and quarreling among you, are you not worldly? Are you not acting like mere men?" (1 Cor. 3:1,3) Yet today it is rare to find *individual congregations* free from jealousy and quarreling, let alone the *city-wide church* as a whole coming together in unity. In many counties, half of the local churches won't even talk to each other (even though they hold to the same theology); and it's all too common for one group to believe that the other group is "dangerous" (especially if these "dangerous" folk are enjoying some degree of blessing). The American Church — that which claims to be born again and walking with the Lord — is incredibly shallow and immature. Yet we think we are so deep.

And what would Paul say about our personality cults? Would he say we were acting like mere men or mighty men? "I gave you milk, not solid food, for you were not yet ready for it. Indeed, you are still not ready. ... For when

one says, 'I follow Paul,' and another, 'I follow Apollos,'
are you not mere men?" (1 Cor. 3:2,4)
And we are far more guilty of this than the Corinthians were.
We are not just followers of men, we are fans of men. We
don't just agree with them, we adore them. Their teachings
carry more weight with us than the Scriptures themselves, and
we base so many of our beliefs on what we have *heard from
men*, not on what we have *learned from the Lord*. There is a
great difference.

It's amazing to see how one national Christian leader can
come up with some new fangled, previously unheard of inter-
pretation of a verse, and before you know it, all his followers
have discovered it! Now they're teaching it as God-given
revelation, and we're devouring this "new truth." But *they*
didn't get it from God. (In all probability their leader didn't
get it from God either.) They got it from man. And we thought
only the Catholic Church claimed to have the infallible inter-
pretation of the Word! Not at all. We have our papal
authorities too — our gifted teachers and anointed prophets
— and *they* can tell us what God really meant to say. How
much more carnal — fleshly, man-centered and utterly human
— can we be? Yet we think we're so spiritual!

Of course, there *is* an important place in the Body for the
teacher of the Word. Teachers are called to feed, build up and
instruct the flock. But they do not take the place of the Holy
Spirit. Many of us are no longer taught by Him!

It's time for us to hear honest words, words that pierce our
complacent crust and unsettle our selfish spirituality. What
Paul prophesied has come about. The time *has* come "when
men will not put up with sound doctrine. *Instead, to suit their
own desires, they will gather around them a great number of
teachers to say what their itching ears want to hear*. They will

turn their ears away from the truth and turn aside to myths" (2 Tim. 4:3-4). The problem with false prophets is that they superficially treat the fracture of God's people saying, "All is well, all is well," while nothing is well (Jer. 6:14). They don't expose the terminal condition of the patient. They offer false hope and security to a dying people and nation. And they say, "No evil can befall us. After all we're the children of God." And so they mislead the masses, because they themselves are misled.

Thank God, many believers today are getting tired of hearing empty words. Reports of success do not fill the growing void. In our hearts, we want the truth, as disturbing and unnerving as it may be. We are sick and tired of human talk. We are determined to hear from the Lord.

What would Jesus say?

Chapter Seven

Slain in the Spirit or Down for the Count

Our Charismatic assemblies are in a lull. Our Full-gospel congregations have stalled. Our Faith churches could be headed for a fall. Where we don't have carnal fanfare we have cold formalism; where we don't have sensationalistic testimonies we have stifling traditions. Our tongues are bland, our prophecies are boring; our interpretations are hollow, our revelations are hokey. We have minor league miracles and mediocre manifestations. Is Jesus exalted by all this?

We give national attention to dramatic "healings" of cancer — after the patient underwent four radical operations and three hellish years of chemotherapy. (Thank God for doctors and medicine, and let's rejoice that the cancer is gone; but healings like this fall far short of the New Testament pattern.) We do special mailings highlighting "incredible miracles" — like a partially disabled man getting out of a wheelchair. But all this is more a cause for great reflecting than for great rejoicing. Instead of giving evidence of our mighty spiritual exploits it gives evidence of our meagerly spiritual accomplishments.

Although *every* healing is important (just ask anyone who has been healed!), would most of our "big" healings be given prominence in the Book of Acts? Were they *national* miracles? With so many dying believers being prayed for throughout the land, with so many totally disabled Christians reading books on faith and healing, is this all we have to praise God for? Oh yes, let's thank the Lord for His grace and rejoice with our brothers and sisters who have been made whole (whether their "miracle" was great or small in our eyes). But let's not act as if we had seen Lazarus raised from the dead. It would embarrass the Holy Spirit. He knows what He can do. And He wants to give us something that will magnify the Lord far more. We have hardly seen anything yet.

Can we put down our defenses for a moment and forget about our critics? Can we stop trying to impress one another and give up our exaggerated talk? Can we quit comparing ourselves to ourselves and be totally candid? What are our services known for? What makes us different as "Spirit-filled" believers? Well, we speak in tongues, prophesy, worship the Lord freely, and have lots of other novelties — like people "being slain" in the Spirit. This is what it's all about! (Permit me to wax sarcastic for a moment. I write these words in love as someone *within* the Pentecostal-Charismatic movement.)

Let's take a look at a typical "Holy Ghost" meeting. First there's some singing and dancing (this is the praise time). Then it gets slower and softer (this is called the worship time. And just think, those non-Charismatics probably don't even know the difference between praise and worship. Look at how much they're missing!). Suddenly it gets really quiet. It's time for a prophetic word, something about God loving us and being pleased with us; and then everybody claps. (Are they applauding the *Lord* for such a nice word, or are they applauding *the one who prophesied* for doing such a good job? Or could it be that they're clapping out of habit? Perish the thought! This is a New Testament church — they do *nothing* out of habit. Everything is led by the Spirit.)

Then it's time for the offering and the announcements. (Isn't it great to see how our services are so unpredictable, spontaneous and brimming with newness and vitality? Thank God we've been delivered from programs and forms!) Then comes the moment we've been waiting for: the message for the hour — something to build us up and make us feel good about ourselves, even if some of us are steeped in sin. After all, this is what Jesus died for, isn't it — to teach us to love ourselves and have a positive self image?

After the message, things really get cooking. There is a prayer line formed for healing. Can you sense the anticipation? The preacher lays hands on each one, and believe it or not, they all start falling! Wow! What a powerful manifestation. The minister laid hands on them, and the Lord laid them out! Some of them can hardly get up. Others lay motionless for minutes. *This is incredible.*

But wait one second. Something is wrong. *Most of the people are sick when they fall — and sick when they get up.* Although the suffering people collapse and shake, the life of God doesn't seem to take. The anointing — or at least what we call the anointing — was strong enough to knock them over, but not strong enough to make them recover. They got their thrill, but they weren't made well. Is *this* the power of God?

Is the Lord now into giving out good feelings instead of good healings? Is this the great manifestation we have been praying for, the awesome demonstration of the might and splendor of the Lord — *people falling into the arms of ushers frantically trying to catch them before they hit the ground?* (Let's not forget the swiftly moving sisters who serve so faithfully in the ministry of towels, draping them over the exposed legs of other sisters who have been slain in the Spirit.)

Yet week after week, in church upon church, the show goes on and on. Some of us are actually excited about all this. Some of us are even puffed up! It's amazing that we've let it go on for so long. Haven't we gotten tired of almost the same script over and over? Isn't it time for something new — or something old?

Consider these reports from the ministry of Maria Woodworth-Etter, the fiery little evangelist who travelled throughout the United States 100 years ago.

In 1899 she held a camp-meeting in Shawnee, Ohio, baptizing the new believers outdoors. This was her description:

"Several thousand people stood on the banks witnessing the solemn scene. The meetings were conducted day and night. People climbed in the trees trying to see. *The Holy Ghost fell like a cyclone, men and women were tossed like as in a wind-storm.* They fell inside and outside the [meeting] house. The police standing outside were frightened, until they were pale. *They said they saw the [meeting] house shaken, like as a storm, by the power of God.* Hundreds were saved. People were convicted for miles around."

In 1885 she was preaching in Indiana. Of her services in and around Tipton she said:

"I never saw such demonstrations of the Spirit and power as at this meeting. Many of the leading church members were struck down or stood held, not able to move, under the power of God, their faces shining with the glory of God. The presence of God was so felt that the fear of the Lord fell upon all the people.

"*For twenty miles round* men and women were struck down in their homes, in business places, and on the roads and streets. Some lay for hours, and had wonderful visions. Many went into the ministry or became evangelists."

From the early 1900's comes this report:

"A few words about the work of God in San Antonio, Texas. The power often came like on Pentecost. *The people were tossed about by the power of God as if by a windstorm, and they seemed light as a feather.* Their faces shone ... It seemed that the Lord took hold of every one that came into the [meeting] house. *Sinners were struck with deep conviction; they began to weep and rush to the altar.* The whole [meeting] house was soon one altar, souls weeping their way to Christ in all parts of the house. ... Ministers all stood like the priests of old; they could not move or work, for the glory and presence of God filled the House of the Lord. *I felt we could not stand it much longer.*"

Sometimes there was judgment:

"A merchant fell in a trance in his home and lay several hours. Hundreds went in to look at him. ... One night there was a party seventeen miles from the city. Some of the young ladies thought they would have some fun; they began to mimic and act out the trance. The Lord struck some of them down. They lay there as if they had been shot. Their fun-making was soon turned into a prayer-meeting, and cries of mercy were heard. ... One man was mocking a woman of whose body God has taken control.

She was preaching with gestures. When in that mocking attitude, God struck him dumb. He became rigid and remained with his hands up, and his mouth drawn in that mocking way for five hours, a gazing-stock for all in the [meeting] house. The fear of God fell on all. They saw it was a fearful thing to mock God or make fun of His work."

Always there were healings:

"Scores of deaf people of all ages were healed — those born deaf, from babies to forty or fifty years of age.

"There was a boy seven years old, had never walked; he was born insane, blind, deaf, and dumb, and always pounding his head and beating himself like the maniac amongst the tombs. They tried everything, including the best medical help, but the doctors could not locate his sufferings, and they said he would never have any sense ... The Lord has performed the greatest miracle ever known ... *this child was born blind, deaf, and dumb, and had no mind; now he can hear and see perfectly. God has given him a bright, intelligent mind; he laughs and plays, and walks around in front of the pulpit every day in view of all the congregation;* before he was healed he had spasms, as many as twenty a day; but now he is well and happy."

"Many were carried in, got up and walked out. The blind shouted for joy; the lame threw away their crutches, and leaped and rejoiced, and said, 'Oh, I am healed!' The deaf and dumb clapped their hands, while tears of joy ran down their faces. Children that had never walked ran about praising the Lord. Some, both young and old people, who were perfectly helpless, received a shock from Heaven's battery, that sent life through their limbs; they clapped their hands and jumped and cried for joy."

"Among the miracles of healing in the first Atlanta meeting, were about ten mutes, some were born deaf and dumb. Among them was a lady who was healed and converted at the same time. She spoke several words of praise right away ... Soon after she brought a friend with her who was born deaf and dumb. They were sitting together. The Holy Ghost took possession of a minister; he spoke several languages and danced and sang in the Spirit, *and then spoke the dumb language in signs.* The message was to the deaf and dumb woman. God took hold of her and her friend brought her to the altar. In a few minutes she was saved and could talk and hear."

Tens of thousands were gloriously converted, many of them over seventy years old. This was the power of Pentecost. What power do we have in our meetings today?

Reinhard Bonkke, the German evangelist presently ministering throughout Africa, reported that for years, whenever he would pray for the baptism of the Spirit, as many as 5000-10,000 believers would simultaneously be slain in the Spirit — and get up speaking in tongues! And he never mentioned a thing about falling nor was anyone there to catch the people. It was an awesome sight to behold.

Another Third World evangelist told of an encounter he had with a leading witch doctor. The man came on the prayer line, cursing and muttering under his breath, but the evangelist had no idea who he was. The local pastors were afraid to even go near him. But when the brother laid hands on him, the witch doctor was hurled about ten feet through the air and pinned to the ground by the power of God. *He rose to his feet delivered.* This is to the glory of the Lord. As for many of our manifestations, how do they glorify Him?

We who claim to be Full-Gospel, Spirit-filled, Charismatic, Word of Faith, or Latter-Rain all see ourselves as the recipients of the great, last-days outpouring, the true heirs of Pentecost.

I wonder: How does God see us?

Chapter Eight

Leaving the Land of Make-Believe

God is invisible. The devil is invisible. Angels and demons are invisible. The entire spirit realm is invisible. *But invisible does not mean unreal.* Yet many of us live in the realm of spiritual make-believe. We mistake fantasy for faith and imagination for inspiration. Our God lives in lullaby land. He is only the Lord of our dreams.

A. W. Tozer explains:

"Since in one of its aspects religion contemplates the invisible, it is easy to understand how it can be erroneously made to contemplate the unreal. The praying man talks of that which he does not see, and fallen human minds tend to assume that what cannot be seen is not of any great importance, and probably not even real, if the truth were known. So religion is disengaged from practical life and retired to the airy region of fancy where dwell the sweet insubstantial nothings which everyone knows do not exist but which they nevertheless lack the courage to repudiate publicly. ... Indeed it is more than possible that the gods

of the heathen are more real to them than is the God of the average Christian."
There are many pagans who would die for their beliefs. Can we live for ours?

Let us make sure that our faith is concrete, producing genuine fruit, since "if our Christianity does not work here where we can test it, it is foolhardy to hope it will successfully transport us into eternity where, if we fail the test, we suffer eternal separation from God" (Francis Frangipane). This it not the time to experiment with religious games! It is time to experience the real God.

Some believers are waiting for the day when they will sit blissfully on a heavenly cloud, mindlessly playing their golden harp. Others have decided not to wait for "heaven." They have already entered into a mindless bliss. What will it take to snap them out of it?

There are many who claim to have great faith. They rebuke demons by the thousands and dispatch angels by the millions. They decree supernatural blessings and impart incredible anointings. But talk is cheap. If so much is happening in the spiritual realm, where is the proof in the natural realm? Where are the overwhelming victories? Which American cities are being overturned for the Lord? Where is the divine visitation?

Paul was fully aware that his opponents could talk. They said: "His letters are weighty and forceful, but in person he is unimpressive and his speaking amounts to nothing" (2 Cor. 10:10). But Paul would not fight words with words. This was his approach:
"I will come to you very soon, if the Lord is willing, and then I will find out not only how these arrogant people

are talking, but what power they have. *For the kingdom of God is not a matter of talk but of power"* (1 Cor. 4:19-20). He is not the God of the theoretical. He is the God of the tangible.

"A God without power to heal a sick heathen's body is a poor recommendation of His ability to save his soul" (John G. Lake). If our God's deeds do not back up His words, how is He different than the other "gods" mankind has created? How do we know that He is not a figure of our own inventing, the product of our wishful thinking? Solomon knew that the Lord alone was God because, as the young king said in prayer,

"You have kept Your promise to Your servant David my father; *with Your mouth You have promised and with Your hand You have fulfilled it — as it is today"* (1 Kin. 8:24).

In 1989 I visited a large church in a large city in the Southeastern United States. The pastor boasted that his congregation had engaged in so much dynamic spiritual warfare that the demonic prince over their city was riddled with holes. In fact, the pastor wondered how this satanic agent was even standing any longer. Yet when I rode up and down the streets of a busy part of that city I was shocked: There was a tremendous increase in worldliness and promiscuity since my last visit there ten years before. Even the pornography industry had greatly taken hold. The devil certainly wasn't aware that he had been defeated.

David Wilkerson relates the all too common story of a discouraged pastor who said,

"My church would stand with me for hours thundering in tongues: binding principalities and powers. We've bound the enemy from the east, west, north and south but the city only gets worse. There is no evidence of a change."

Yet we make so many excuses, anything to evade the facts! We say:

"The breakthrough was about to come, it was right around the corner." (In other words, "We have never seen anything happen, but at least this way we can remain optimistic!")

Or: "You needed to see the victory through the eyes of faith. You can't be so carnally minded!" (In other words, "Because there is no tangible evidence that anything actually took place, we'll just say it did.")

Or: "Brother, you didn't realize that we were fighting demons of cosmic proportions. This was an unusually huge battle." (In other words, "It can't possibly be that we had so little success pulling down strongholds over our town of 1000 people. We must be situated right in the center of one of Satan's strategic locations." How amazing that so many of us find ourselves in the midst of critical battles with leading demonic forces!)

But when God's power is manifested in the demolition, destruction and devastation of demonic fortresses, no excuses are necessary. The crushing conquest speaks for itself.

"The weapons we fight with are not the weapons of the world. On the contrary they have divine power to demolish strongholds. We demolish arguments and every pretension that sets itself up against God, and we take captive every thought to make it obedient to Christ" (2 Cor. 10:4-5).

We may have to persevere in faith and shut our ears to the lies of the enemy. We may have to steadfastly refuse to cave in when the going gets rough and the results seem discouraging. But if we do not faint or collapse, if we are not intimidated by the pressures of the battle, we will experience triumph and victory in the Lord. He is a Man of War.

Here is an example of spiritual warfare that works, related earlier this century by John G. Lake:

"In South Africa some years ago in a single night a fever epidemic struck the country for three hundred and fifty miles. As I rode through a section of that area, I found men dead in their beds beside their wives; children dead in their beds alongside the living; whole families stricken, dying, and some dead. In one single month one-fourth of the entire population of that district, both white and black died. We had to organize an army to dig graves, and an army of men to make caskets. We could not buy wood enough in that section of the country to make caskets, so we buried them in a blanket, or without a blanket, when it was necessary to save the blankets for a better purpose.

"I had a man in my company whom God anointed to pray as I never found anybody else anointed to pray. For days he remained under a thorn tree, and when I passed in the morning I would hear his voice in prayer, and when I returned in the evening I would hear his voice in prayer. Many times I got a prepared meal and carried it to him and aroused him long enough to get him to eat it. I would ask, 'Brother, how is it? Are you getting through?' He would reply, 'Not yet.' But one day he said, 'Mr. Lake, I feel today that if I had just a little help in faith that my spirit would go through to God.' And I went on my knees beside him, joined my heart with his, and voiced my prayer to God.

"As we prayed, the Spirit of the Lord overwhelmed our souls and presently I found myself, not kneeling under the tree, but moving gradually away from the tree, some fifty or one hundred feet. My eyes gradually opened, and I witnessed such a scene as I never witnessed before — a multitude of demons like a flock of sheep! The Spirit had come upon him also, and he rushed ahead of me, cursing that army of demons, and they were driven back to hell, or the place from whence they came. *Beloved, the next morning when we awoke, that epidemic of fever was gone.* That is the power of divine healing — God destroying Satan."

In Richmond, Virginia in 1986, an experienced intercessor gathered together all the pastors and believers who were willing to join him for early morning prayer. At the time Richmond had the highest per capita murder rate in the country, averaging one homicide a day. After a couple of weeks of prayer, the group attacked the "strong man" over the city: murder and violence. *For the next twenty-eight days no one was murdered in Richmond.* The Spirit had muzzled the enemy. God had shut him down! A high ranking police official wrote to one of the local newspapers. He didn't know what forces were responsible for the remarkable change, but he urged them to keep it up!

Unfortunately, enthusiasm for unified morning prayer soon waned — and eventually the murder rate jumped back up. But for everyone who had eyes to see, the proof was all too clear: When the people of God come together as one, when they unite their wills with His will, when they humble themselves before His throne and call on the infinite resources of heaven — something tremendous takes place! But what does all our noise accomplish? What do our empty proclamations produce? The angels of God recognize the true empowering. *So do the demons of hell.*

When Jesus was teaching on the Sabbath in Capernaum,
"a man in their synagogue who was possessed by an evil spirit cried out, 'What do you want with us, Jesus of Nazareth? Have You come to destroy us? *I know who You are — the Holy One of God!*' " (Mark 1:23-24)

After the Sabbath, "when the sun was setting, the people brought to Jesus all who had various kinds of sickness, and laying His hands on each one, He healed them. Moreover, demons came out of many people, shouting, 'You are the Son of God!' But He rebuked them and would not allow them to speak, because *they knew He was the Messiah*" (Luke 4:40-41).

When Paul became troubled at the harassment coming through a demonized slave girl at Philippi, "he turned around and said to the spirit, 'In the name of Jesus Christ I command you to come out of her!' *At that moment the spirit left her*" (Acts 16:18). But when the seven sons of Sceva in Ephesus tried to use the same method, they were in for a surprise:

"They would say, 'In the name of Jesus, whom Paul preaches, I command you to come out. ... [But] the evil spirit answered them, *'Jesus I know, and I know about Paul, but who are you?'* Then the man who had the evil spirit jumped on them and overpowered them all. He gave them such a beating that they ran out of the house naked and bleeding" (Acts 19:13-16).
Seven men brutalized by only one!

Just think: When the demons saw Jesus, they pleaded with Him not to torture or destroy them. "Jesus, please don't hurt us!" When Paul exercised the authority of the Savior's name, the spirit in the slave girl had to instantly obey. But when the sons of Sceva sought to use the name of One they knew of but did not follow, *they* got hurt badly — to their shame and humiliation.

There is an important lesson to be learned: It is one thing to speak forth the name of Jesus and declare His Word. It is another thing to be clothed with His character and do His Word. Wouldn't it be wonderful if we could truly be "living epistles" so that when Satan *read* us he would run? Wouldn't it be glorious if demons saw us coming and, with trembling voices said, "I know who you are!"

"Submit yourselves, then, to God" — that is where it all begins. "Resist the devil, [not just with your mouth, but with your heart, your mind, your actions, your very self,] and he will flee from you" (James 4:7). Our antics won't chase the devil away. *The holy anointing will.* In the words of Francis Frangipane:

"Victory begins with the name of Jesus on our lips. It is consummated by the nature of Jesus in our hearts." *He* is our strength and our song. "Crown Him. Follow Him. Fight under Him" (G. Campbell Morgan).

This is how we wage — and win — the war.

God called Joshua to be strong and courageous. But it was not just because he had to fight the giants in the land of Canaan. It was not simply because he had to assail mighty nations with his outmanned army. No. The outward struggle was only part of the battle. The real test was obedience to God:

"Be strong and resolute, for you shall apportion to this people the land that I swore to their fathers to give them. *But you must be very strong and resolute to observe faithfully all the Teaching that My servant Moses enjoined upon you.* Do not deviate from it to the right or to the left, that you may be successful wherever you go (Josh. 1:6-7, New Jewish Version).

The truly triumphant believer is the one who fully obeys.

It is exhilarating to talk about cosmic victories and strategize about our international ministry plans. But there is one sure way to test our authority. Are we defeating the enemy in our families and homes? Are we "more than conquerors" when it comes to subduing the desires of our bodies and minds? Are we masters or are we slaves of the flesh?

"The severest battles of a man's life are fought out in secret and in his own individual soul. Temptation to evil in its varied forms comes far more subtly to a man when he is alone than when he is with others. I begin my fight inside; in the secret recesses of my inner life, in the hall of the imagination, in the chamber of the affections, there the fight must first be fought. ... The fiercest battles of the individual life, the longest, the most strenuous, are the battles fought in absolute loneliness" (Campbell Morgan). How are we faring there?

It is time for us to leave the land of make-believe. We are either walking in divine authority or we are not. We are either dominating the darkness or the darkness is dominating us. We are either winning the battle or losing. We can't fool God. We can't fool the devil.

Why continue to fool ourselves?

Chapter Nine

Prayer Is Mightier than the Pen

War is savage. Cruel weapons kill and disfigure. Atomic bombs decimate whole cities. Bullets and shrapnel shatter bones and rip through flesh. Swords pierce and slash and maim. Yet "the pen is mightier than the sword."

The written word has done more to shape history than the smiting sword. Just a few short books have had a greater impact on humanity than all the battles that have ever been fought. The Koran has brought more people under its influence than have the combined efforts of Muslim military might. Luther's "95 Theses" nailed to a church door in Germany shook Europe more than many armies. Einstein's little formula scrawled on a piece of paper, $e = mc^2$, was the real detonating force of the hydrogen bomb.

Yet there is something far more powerful than the pen, and that is *prayer*. In fact, the key to true power is perseverance in private prayer. Prayer prevails. Prayer produces. Prayer is preeminent. God calls us to persistent prayer.

Prayer opens up the heavens: "When all the people were being baptized, Jesus was baptized too. *And as He was praying*, heaven was opened and the Holy Spirit descended on Him in bodily form like a dove" (Luke 3:21-22).

Prayer transforms: Jesus "took Peter, John and James with Him and went up onto a mountain to pray. *As He was praying*, the appearance of His face changed, and His clothes became as bright as a flash of lightning" (Luke 9:28-29).

Prayer gets resounding results: "*After they prayed*, the place where they were meeting was shaken. And they were all filled with the Holy Spirit and spoke the word of God boldly" (Acts 4:31).

Could it be that we need more prayer? "Those who have left the deepest impression on this sin-cursed earth have been men and women of prayer" (D. L. Moody).

"*Pray* in the Spirit on *all occasions* with *all kinds* of prayers and requests" (Eph. 6:18).

"Jesus told His disciples a parable to show them that they should *always pray* and *not give up*" (Luke 18:1).

"God, whom I serve with my whole heart in preaching the gospel of His Son, is my witness how *constantly I remember you in my prayers at all times*" (Rom. 1:9-10).

"As for me, far be it from me that I should sin against the Lord *by failing to pray for you*" (1 Sam. 12:23).

"I thank God, whom I serve, as my forefathers did, with a clear conscience, *as night and day I constantly remember you in my prayers*" (2 Tim. 1:3).

"*Pray continually*" (1 Thess. 5:17).

This is the Word of the Lord!

Jesus needed to pray. "One of those days Jesus went out to a mountainside to pray, and *spent the night praying to God.*

Very early in the morning, while it was still dark, Jesus got up, left the house and went off to a solitary place, *where He prayed.*" Many times "crowds of people came to hear Him and to be healed of their sicknesses. *But Jesus often withdrew to lonely places and prayed"* (Luke 6:12; Mark 1:35; Luke 5:15-16). The Son of God gave Himself to prayer, not *in spite* of the crowds, but *because* of the crowds. Without prayer, even He could do nothing. Prayer was His lifeline to the Father.

Peter needed to pray. This was his pattern before the Spirit fell: "When they arrived [in Jerusalem], they went upstairs to the upper room where they were staying. ... *They all joined together constantly in prayer"* (Acts 1:13-14). After he was Spirit-immersed, his habit didn't change. When the grieving disciples brought Peter into the room where Tabitha (Dorcas) was laid, he "sent them all out of the room; *then he got down on his knees and prayed.* Turning toward the dead woman, he said, 'Tabitha, get up.' She opened her eyes, and seeing Peter she sat up" (Acts 9:40-41). He knew where his true strength was found.

Paul needed to pray. When he was struck down on the road to Damascus, he was blind for three days, eating and drinking nothing. What was he doing? "The Lord told [Ananias], 'Go to the house of Judas on Straight Street and ask for a man from Tarsus named Saul, *for he is praying"* (Acts 9:11). Throughout his many years of ministry, he never graduated from the school of prayer: "[Publius'] father was sick in bed, suffering from fever and dysentery. Paul went in to see him and, *after prayer,* placed his hands on him and healed him" (Acts 28:8).

We are no better than Jesus, Peter or Paul. *We need to pray.* When we concentrate in prayer, things happen. Yet we are so often lax and distracted! Moody Stuart had three rules for prayer. Most of us have not yet mastered the first one: "*Pray till you pray.*" (The other rules were: "Pray till you are conscious of being heard; pray till you receive the answer.") Have you ever spent an hour in prayer without even praying ten minutes?

We find it hard to focus our attention on God and keep our thoughts from wandering. That's why Peter exhorted his flock to be "clear minded and self-controlled *so that you can pray*" (1 Pet. 4:7). But we do not take prayer seriously enough. We often pray out of a sense of obligation, to complete the requirements on our daily spiritual "checklist." We try to fit prayer in, or we pray so as to not fall away. For many of us, just finding time to pray is the great struggle. But Jesus took for granted that we would pray ("*When* you pray ..."). That is not so much where the battle should be. *Fervent prayer is the battle.*

James tells us that "Elijah was a man just like us" (James 5:17). He had the same weaknesses we have; he went through the same battles we do. He had to fight the flesh and overcome weakness and fear. But he took hold of God and would not let go. "He prayed earnestly that it would not rain, and it did not rain on the land for three and a half years" (James 5:17). Forty-two months of drought! The prayers of one righteous servant literally impacted the whole nation. Every man, woman and child — from the palace of the king to the lowest dungeon — was effected. Just think of the power of prayer! A solitary prophet cried out to the Maker and Keeper of heaven and earth — and the Lord Almighty listened to his voice! God listens to our voice too. *Isn't it amazing that we can know so much about prayer yet pray so little, and with so little fervor and faith?*

As for Elijah, his prayer battle was not over. He stood on the mountain and put his life on the line. He prayed with passion and the fire came down: "Answer me, O Lord, answer me, so these people will know that You, O Lord, are God, and that You are turning their hearts back again" (1 Kin. 18:37). He was absorbed; he was caught up in prayer. And the nation was shaken again. The fire fell on the sacrifices and the people fell on the ground. The Lord was exalted and the false prophets were executed. What an incredible, stirring event! *God responds to fervent prayer — from Elijah, from you, from me — as long as our hearts are pure.* Yet there is still more to Elijah's prayer vigil.

"Again he prayed, and the heavens gave rain, and the earth produced its crops" (James 5:18). This time the torrents came. Elijah had not offered up a flippant request. He had not simply made a casual petition. Prayers like that don't even reach the ceiling — let alone ascend to God's throne. *Elijah prayed with intensity.* And he prayed until he prayed through. First he told the godless king, "Go, eat and drink, for there is the sound of abundance of rain" (1 Kin. 18:41). But Elijah was speaking by faith: There wasn't a cloud in the sky! Now the test had come. So "Elijah climbed to the top of Carmel, bent down to the ground and put his face between his knees" (1 Kin. 18:42). He got away from the crowds and the noise, crouching down in the labor pains of prophetic prayer. He shut off all outside distractions, and he cried out to the Lord.

" 'Go and look toward the sea,' he told his servant. And he went up and looked. 'There is nothing there,' he said." But Elijah wouldn't — and couldn't — stop. "*Seven times* Elijah said, 'Go back.' " (1 Kin. 18:43). Seven times he crouched down and prayed. Six times the sky was clear. And then — one more heart cry, one more groan, one more, "Answer me, O Lord!"

— and there was a small cloud ... a black sky ... a rising wind
... and *heavy* rain.

Oh that we would persevere in prayer! How many times
do we cave in and give up? — just when the heavens are about
to burst; just when the answer is about to come; just when the
devil whispers, "There's no hope;" just when our minds say,
"Enough." Real praying power means real staying power. We
must discipline ourselves to endure. Some of us *do* live in a
fantasy world, believing that the answer will come tomorrow,
while we do nothing to make it happen today. But for others,
the breakthrough really is near — if only we will not quit!

"Believe me, to pray with all your heart and strength,
with the reason and the will, to believe vividly that God
will listen to your voice through Christ, and, verily, to do
the thing He pleaseth thereupon — this is the last, the
greatest achievement of the Christian's warfare upon
earth. *Teach us to pray, O Lord*" (Coleridge).

Jacob Boehme said that "to pray aright is right earnest
work," and in the words of David MacIntyre, "Prayer is the
most sublime energy of which the spirit of man is capable."
That's why Paul could ask the Romans to join him in his ministry *struggle* by *praying* for him (Rom. 15:30). That's why he
could tell the Colossians that Epaphras, a *fellow soldier* in the
faith, was always *wrestling* in prayer for them (Col. 4:12). These
are graphic terms: "fellow soldier ... wrestling." Prayer can
be violent and fierce! It is really the ultimate fight.

Jesus won His war through prayer. (This is a thought that
is almost overwhelming to consider. Still and all, it is true.)
"During the days of Jesus' life on earth, He offered up prayers
and petitions *with loud cries and tears* to the One who could
save Him from death, and He was heard because of His

reverent submission" (Heb. 5:7). Let us battle, let us grapple in prayer.

This is the way to break through. Pour out your heart, unburden your soul, plead your case — and your Father will hear. Persuade God to do what He has promised and desires to do. Give Him no rest until He responds. (I am speaking in human terms.) Remind Him of His Word and His reputation. Convince Him of the urgent pressing need. Show Him that you are sincere. Do all this in accordance with His will and the answer will be on the way!

"O Lord, God of heaven, the great and awesome God, who keeps His covenant of love with those who love Him and obey His commands, let Your ear be attentive and Your eyes open to hear the prayer Your servant is praying day and night ..." (Neh. 1:5-6).

Nehemiah meant what he prayed. And the Lord heeded his plea.

Many parts of China today are experiencing great revival. Yet this move of God did not spring up from nowhere. The Chinese saints from decades past toiled, labored and sowed. But who brought the gospel to them? It was men and women like Jonathan and Rosalind Goforth, who built on the efforts of people like J. Hudson Taylor, *who built on the prayers of people like William C. Burns.* How many have heard of Burns today? Yet the very angels knew him by name. He was a prominent preacher for nine years in Scotland where he saw the Spirit poured out. Then he left home for good and labored in obscurity; but his prayers were like seeds sown deep in the ground. Years later, the fruit appeared.

Charles Finney also experienced many dynamic answers to prayer. He gave himself faithfully to intercession, and the

Lord gave him faithful intercessors. (If you are in the ministry and you want more prayer warriors, just do what he did. Give yourself to more warring prayer.) This is what Finney learned:

"Now, do not deceive yourselves with thinking that you offer effectual prayer, unless you have this intense desire for the blessing. I do not believe in it. *Prayer is not effectual unless it is offered up with an agony of desire.* The apostle Paul speaks of it as a travail of the soul. Jesus Christ, when He was praying in the garden, was in such an agony that 'His sweat was as it were great drops of blood falling down to the ground' (Luke 22:44). I have never known a person sweat blood; but I have known a person [to] pray till the blood started from his nose. And I have known a person [to] pray till they were all wet with perspiration, in the coldest weather in winter. I have known persons [to] pray for hours, till their strength was all exhausted with the agony of their minds [souls]. Such prayers prevailed with God." *Fervent prayer is the victory.*

"When prayer rises to its true level, self, with its concerns and needs, is for the time forgotten, and the interests of Christ fill, and sometimes overwhelm, the soul. It is then that prayer becomes most urgent and intense. ... Livingstone reports of Robert Bruce that in prayer 'every sentence was like a strong bolt shot up to heaven.' The biographer of Richard Baxter tells us that when he gathered his spirit together to pray, it 'took wing to heaven.' And it is related in similar terms of Archbishop Leighton that 'his manner of praying was so earnest and importunate as proved that his soul mounted up to God in the flame of his own aspirations' " (MacIntyre).

Finney describes a man who prayed "as if he would do violence to Heaven, and then [I] have seen the blessing come as plainly in answer to his prayer as if it were revealed, so that no person would doubt it any more than if God had spoken from heaven. ... Blessed man! He was the reproach of the ungodly, and of carnal, unbelieving professors [of the faith]; but he was the favourite of Heaven, and a prevailing prince in prayer."

Fervent prayer was a key to the great soul-winning success of the early Salvation Army:

"Prayer is agony of soul, a wrestling of the spirit. You know how men and women deal with one another when they are in desperate earnestness for something to be done. That is prayer, whether it be to man or to God; and when you get your heart influenced and melted and wrought up and burdened by the Holy Ghost for souls, you will have power, and you will never pray but somebody will be convinced, some poor soul's dark eyes will be opened and spiritual life will commence" (Catherine Booth).

"You must pray with all your might. That does not mean saying your prayers, or sitting gazing about in church or chapel with eyes wide open, while someone else says them for you. It means fervent, effectual, untiring wrestling with God. It means that grappling with Omnipotence, that clinging to Him, following Him about, so to speak, day and night, as the widow did the unjust judge, with agonizing pleadings and arguments and entreaties, until the answer comes and the end is gained. ... If you mean to succeed you must shut your ears and eyes to all but what God has said, and hold Him to His word: and you cannot do this in any sleepy mood; you cannot be a prevailing Israel unless you wrestle as Jacob wrestled, regardless of time or aught else, save obtaining the blessing sought — that is, you must pray with your might" (William Booth).

It is not fleshly emotionalism or wild fanaticism that prevails. It is focused faith and concentrated concern. It is praying with spiritual intensity. It is making contact with God and staying in contact with God. *Fervent prayer — and more of it — is the key.* Just think how the world would be affected if we prayed with fervor and prayed more!

Of course, more prayer is *not* the key if by more prayer we just mean asking the Lord to add something extra to us. That alone will not do. We have departed too far from the roots of the faith. Our present walks with the Lord are leading most of us around in circles, and our personal *foundations* are often faulty. We need more than just building up!

But, if by more prayer we mean ceasing to rely on ourselves, crucifying the plans of the natural mind, coming to the end of our own resources, spending hours in God's presence to become like Him, and asking Him to change us and rearrange us, to awake us and remake us, to act and move on our behalf, then more prayer is the key.

"Lord God we are rending our hearts! Will *You* rend the heavens and come down? Visit us with Your holy fire, Lord God! We are utterly dependent on You — and You are utterly dependable. Answer us, O Lord, answer us — for the sake of Your great name, for the sake of Your hungry people, and for the sake of Your dying world."

God Himself will be the Answer to our prayers.

Can we ask for anything less?

Chapter Ten

Hi-Tech Believers and a Push-Button God

Where would we be today without instant formulas —
those marvelous time-saving methods that provide shortcuts
for everything from quick weight loss to immediate financial
success, from learning a foreign language in two weeks to
building a happy marriage in ten days? It used to be that
spiritual *maturity* also took years to develop. But not anymore
— we've discovered heaven's secret techniques for this too!
Just put them into practice, and you'll be a giant overnight.
After all, this *is* the nuclear age. Shoudn't we get modern with
our faith?

What is the essence of the microwave mentality? Instant
results with no preparation. *Today we have microwave ministry.*

We train believers how to "operate in divine healing" —
but they are lacking the compassion of the Lord. We raise up
skilled "soulwinners" — but they do not weep for the lost. We
hold workshops on "how to prophesy" — but we fail to emphasize the importance of sharing God's burden out of a

broken heart. We teach people how to "bind the devil" —
while they themselves are bound. We equip believers with the
latest techniques of spiritual warfare — when they haven't
even conquered the lusts of the flesh. We have seminars on
the gifts of the Spirit — but we have forgotten that His name
is HOLY. *He does not like being associated with defiled vessels.* "First clean the inside of the cup and dish, and then the
outside also will be clean" (Matt. 23:26). But we have emphasized the outward! We are more "Pharisaical" than we
know.

We have bypassed the cross with its death to ego, catering
instead to man's lust for power, excitement and prestige. But
this is not the way God's kingdom works. Through His Son,
He makes us His relatives — not His agents. *His family members are to bear His marks, not be His manipulators.*

Yet many of our teachers seem to lead us in the way of
spiritual manipulation: "Just learn the laws of the Spirit; put
the Word to work for yourself; enter into your full inheritance
— and rule and reign as you please. You call the shots with
God. He'll do your bidding for you" — as if the Almighty
Creator were some celestial bell-hop at the beck and call of
His redeemed servants! *May the Lord have mercy on us.*

No! There are no shortcuts with God — no techniques that
will allow us to slip by without passing the tests. And while
there are some believers who have had apparent overnight
success without the proving of their character — their churches growing up in a few short years and their ministries filled
with all kinds of supernatural gifts — God will not be mocked.
Those who have not built right — because they themselves
were not built right — will see their great works fall as quickly
as they rose. God may give them an abundance of outward
blessing, just like He gave the Israelites quail in the desert:

"But while the meat was still between their teeth and before it could be consumed, the anger of the Lord burned against the people, and He struck them with a plague" (Num. 11:33).

One time Moses did things his way — and still got miraculous results. Instead of speaking to the rock as God commanded, Moses struck it twice and harshly rebuked the people. *The water still flowed out,* but it cost Moses the Promised Land (Num. 20). Could it be that some leaders who are blatantly doing things their way — and still getting results for now — are forfeiting their reward in the process?

Today, there are ministers who think they have learned to push the right spiritual buttons, generating miracles and manifestations galore. But if their lives are marked by arrogance, unteachability and a desire to be somebody big in the kingdom, a "plague" is already upon them. *They are sitting ducks for the devil.* That is why so many who seemed so powerful are falling so pitifully — they have no more defense against the enemy. They have taken matters into their own hands. *They hardly need the Lord anymore.* What a tragedy we are witnessing in this day.

We protest that prayer has been taken out of our schools. But many times we have taken God out of our prayers! We often forget to humbly *ask* — to make our requests known to the Lord. We are too busy making positive confessions, or commanding, decreeing, declaring, binding, loosing and imparting. You would almost think that all this would take God's breath away. We think we're so dynamic. The Lord knows we're deluded. He is certainly not amused with our "exploits of faith."

Intercession means asking on behalf of others, standing in their place before God and against the devil. But we have made it into a space-age spiritual science and a high-tech prayer procedure. Only the elite pray right. You almost get the impression that the saints of old hardly knew how to intercede, since they hadn't heard our latest tapes! Have we forgotten that true prayer is not based on formulas but on fellowship? Prayer is entering into *communion* with our heavenly Father and being *intimate* with Him. *This is something that demands our all* — our hearts, our souls, our minds.

Yet we are often cursed with such a careless attitude! We hardly realize the sacred ground we are standing on when we approach the throne of God. Through prayer we enter the holiest place in the entire spiritual universe, the innermost sanctuary of the Lord. He expects us to give Him our undivided attention. *He gives us His.* The King deserves respect — not some lightweight babbling.

Here too we have strayed. We have prostituted one of the most precious gifts the Spirit has given us: the ability to pray in a heavenly tongue. It has become our all-purpose answer for everything — faster than a speeding bullet, more piercing than a laser beam, accomplishing awesome things around the world — while we think about balancing our checkbooks, cleaning the house, catching up on our reading, or making vacation plans. Isn't this great? All we have to do is keep our mouths moving, and God takes care of the rest! Some of us are really advanced: We have learned to handle our daily business while at the same time speaking incessantly in tongues. Talk about redeeming the time! Why pray and think together — when our spirits can deal with the heavenly while our heads are busy with the earthly? But there are no shortcuts to prayer either. Abraham and Moses had something we still need: friendship with a God who cared.

Prayer is not some mindless repetition of religious mumbo-jumbo — whether it's praying the rosary or speaking in tongues. In fact, five hours of praying in tongues will get us no closer to God than saying a thousand "Hail Mary's" unless our tongues flow out of faith toward God and love toward man. Without faith, not even the Word of God profits us (Heb. 4:2), and without love, all of our "praying in the Spirit" sounds like "a resounding gong or a clapping cymbal" (1 Cor. 13:1). It is just a lot of noise!

Prayer is not a matter of mechanical mindless muttering. Prayer springs from our relationship with a Person, not from our rote performance of religious rites. When we are in harmony with the God we pray to (whether or not we fully understand everything we are saying), the sweet sound of our heavenly tongues can fill heaven with its fragance — and shake the very foundations of hell. John G. Lake said that praying in tongues was the making of his life, and Jackie Pullinger, who has served for many years in the treacherous walled city of Hong Kong, saw very little ministry success — until she began to pray consistently in other tongues. Then the Spirit began to work — and no one works like Him. Hundreds and hundreds of hardened Chinese criminals and gang members, all hopelessly addicted to heroine or opium, were completely delivered with no withdrawal pains as they called on the Lord, were filled with His Spirit — and prayed in a brand new tongue.

But men and women like John Lake in the past, and Jackie Pullinger today, are no strangers to the crucified life. They are hungry for God, not for gimmicks — for His presence, not for a performance. Jesus alone — not some big impressive show — brings fulfillment to people like them. The Lord's purpose for us is a *relationship* — not *robotic results*.

Yet we have even put the eternal salvation of a human soul — there is *nothing* more personal than this — into a package: "Raise your hand, come forward, repeat this prayer with me — and now you're a child of God." What would happen if we were told: "No formulas allowed! Bring people into a *relationship* with the Lord." Would we feel helpless? Would we lose our only "evidence" that people were born again? Would we even know how to introduce them to Jesus our living Savior? But this is the day of fax machines and overnight delivery. Who has time to wait for true conversions and genuine repentance?

And so our innovations continue. There's even a new substitute for reading the Word: Just listen to subliminal Bible tapes! Your conscious mind doesn't hear the Scriptures, but your inner man takes it all in. This way you can actually grow in faith while you sleep! And yet Smith Wigglesworth raised the dead, drove out cancer from the sick and dying, and lifted many invalids from their wheelchairs — without any of our quick-fix gimmicks. He didn't even have the Bible on computer. (There's nothing wrong with computerized Bibles, but for many it will be a trap: With the Word of God stored on their hard drives, they will no longer store it in their hearts.) Could it be God is saying, "Enough!"?

Improved "technology" is *not* the key to the blessing of God. In the words of Leonard Ravenhill, "We have plenty of equipment but not much enduement." Advanced formulas are *not* the solution we are looking for. The Church does not need to make any more new discoveries! "Back to the basics" is the word for today.

It will also be the word for tomorrow.

Chapter Eleven

Repentance: The Missing Jewel

There is hardly anything more fundamental to the life of a believer than repentance: hardly anything more life giving, more liberating, more glorious. That's why the devil has sought to discredit it. Mention repentance to most believers and immediately they think of condemnation, brow beating, negativity, judgmentalism and death. Nothing could be farther from the truth. Repentance is a *gift* from God. Without it, sinners can not be regenerated and saints can not be renewed. It is a wonder of God's infinite grace. *Only the imperfect are candidates for it.*

Repentance is exclusively for those: who have fallen short; who acknowledge their need; who have turned away; who have sinned; who want to come back. It is not for the totally righteous or self-sufficient. They do not qualify for such a precious gem! Nor do they know what they are missing.

Repentance is God's activating grace. It remakes and restores and repairs. It is the essential step to redemption. It starts in darkness and ends in light. It starts in bondage and ends in freedom. It starts in death and ends in life. It makes the unclean clean and the unholy holy. It makes the difference between heaven and hell. *God only forgives those who repent.*

True repentance, the fruit of godly sorrow, "leads to salvation and leaves no regret" (2 Cor. 7:10). God's heavenly kingdom is filled with repentant sons and daughters of Adam, those who have sorrowed for their sins and found pardon. *They will never sorrow again.* John Milton was right when he described repentance as, "the golden key that opens the palace of eternity." Yet the gates of God's kingdom are shut to those who refuse to repent. They can never enter in. They must do without salvation — and they will have much to regret. They cast off godly sorrow in this life, and they will have the sorrow of this world in the life to come. How tragic! We cannot afford to pass over repentance.

Repentance is the most basic of the basics, the very first of "the elementary teachings of Christ" (Heb. 6:1). It is the special property of the human race: *Of all God's creation, only man can repent.* That's why "there is rejoicing in the presence of the angels of God over one sinner who repents" (Luke 15:10). It is a thrilling sight for them to behold! That's why the early believers, all of them Jews, praised God because He had granted "even the Gentiles repentance unto life" (Acts 11:18). This was their way in to the inheritance. In fact, one reason Jesus has not yet returned is this: He is waiting for more people to repent! "The Lord is not slow in keeping His promise, as some understand slowness. He is patient with you, not wanting anyone to perish, but everyone to come to *repentance*" (2 Pet. 3:9). It is repent or perish. *Repentance means being saved from our sins.*

The Scriptures speak of "repentance unto life" and "repentance unto salvation." There is nothing negative about that! In fact, repentance is only for those the Lord has not rejected: "Those who I love I rebuke and discipline. *So be earnest, and repent.* I stand at the door and knock ..." (Rev. 3:19-20). Praise God when He knocks at our door! We are about to experience mercy and grace — if we humble ourselves and repent.

Look at how David responded when Nathan the prophet exposed the king's sin. (*This* is the first step to repentance — having our sin laid open and brought to light. Who wants to have cancer in his spirit and not even know about it? Thank God when uncleanness is revealed! Consider these words of wisdom: "Before God can deliver us, we must undeceive ourselves" [Ambrose]; "The greatest of all faults is to be conscious of none" [Thomas Carlyle]; "Self-knowledge is the first condition of repentance" [Oswald Chambers].)

First, David appealed for mercy, pure and simple: "Have mercy on me, O God, according to Your unfailing love." He cast Himself wholly on the goodness of God. He dove into the ocean of grace: "According to Your great compassion, blot out my transgressions."

What a fantastic request. David comes with his *transgressions*, his *iniquity*, and his *sin*. He is filthy and vile and stained. Yet he appeals to his holy God's unfailing love and great compassion. And the Lord is pleased with this! He invites it, He welcomes it, He desires it. He wants to make us whole. He doesn't want to hide His face from *us*. He wants to hide His face from *our sin*.

"Who is a God like You, who pardons sins and forgives the transgression of the remnant of His inheritance? You do not stay angry forever [Hallelujah!] but delight to show mercy. [Read this again: *God delights to show mercy.*] You

will again have compassion on us; You will tread our sins underfoot and hurl all our iniquities into the depths of the sea" (Mic. 7:18-19).
This is the God we approach.

Look at the boldness of David's repentance: The man who committed adultery and arranged for cold blooded murder, the one who disappointed and offended the Lord now asks that his evil would be *blotted out* and *washed away*, that he would be *cleansed* until he is *whiter than snow*, that *gladness* and *rejoicing* would be restored to him, that God would create for him a *pure heart* and renew a *steadfast spirit* within him, and that the Lord would open his lips so that his tongue could *sing God's righteousness* and his mouth *declare God's praise*. Amazing!

What an incredible exchange. He comes with iniquity. He leaves with purity. He comes with guilt. He leaves with pardon. He comes weighed down. He leaves rejoicing. We serve a compassionate God!

But repentance is not cheap. It cost Jesus His life blood. It brought Him down to the depths. He paid the price to ransom our lives. He suffered that we might be changed. "He Himself bore our sins in His body on the tree, so that we might *die to sins and live for righteousness*" (1 Pet. 2:24). Repentance is where it begins. We die to the old and embrace the new; we turn from the world and turn to the Lord. It is rebirth, it is salvation, it is new life. *If we continue to live as we did before, then we should question our salvation — and question our repentance.* Jesus did not die in vain.

"Christ's blood avails nothing except in so far as it brings you near to the Father of your spirits. Christ's blood is just a holy path to a holy nature" (William C. Burns).

Speaking of His disciples, the Lord said, "For them I sanctify Myself, that they too may be truly sanctified" (John 17:19). He set Himself apart to His Father — every second of every day He lived on this earth — that we would be set apart too. "Both the One who makes men holy and those who are made holy are of the same family. So Jesus is not ashamed to call them brothers" (Heb. 2:11). His Father is our Father too.

John taught us that, "Everyone who sins breaks the law." But Jesus "appeared so that He might *take away our sins*. And in Him is no sin." Therefore: "No one who lives in Him keeps on sinning. No one who continues to sin has either seen Him or known Him." Could anything be more clear? "He who does what is sinful is of the devil." But, "the reason the Son of God appeared was to *destroy the devil's work*." Therefore: "No one who is born of God will continue to sin, because God's seed remains in him; he cannot go on sinning, because he has been born of God" (1 John 3:4-9). Whoever has been born of God has received a new nature. The core of his being is different. It is "conversion" in the truest sense of the word. *Conversion means revolution and change.*

The Roman believers used to be slaves to sin. "But [wrote Paul,] now that you have been set free from sin and have becomes slaves to God, the benefit you reap leads to holiness, and the result is eternal life" (Rom. 6:22). They were no longer the same.

The Corinthians were once guilty of every kind of vice. But not any more! "... you were washed, you were sanctified, you were justified in the name of the Lord Jesus Christ and by the Spirit of our God" (1 Cor. 6:11). They were not even to eat with so-called believers who walked in the old ways of the flesh. The days of gross sin were behind them.

To the Ephesians it was written: "For you were once darkness, but now you are children of light in the Lord. Live as children of light" (Eph. 5:8). There was no way around the simple facts: The saved were to be as different from the unsaved as day is from night.

"God is light; in Him there is no darkness at all. If we claim to have fellowship with Him yet walk in the darkness, we lie and do not live by the truth. But if we walk in the light, as He is in the light, we have fellowship with one another, and the blood of Jesus, His Son, purifies us from all sin" (1 John 1:5-7).
There is no middle ground.

Paul reminded Titus:
"At one time we too were foolish, disobedient, deceived and enslaved by all kinds of passions and pleasures. We lived in malice and envy, being hated and hating one another. But when the kindness and love of God our Savior appeared [something great took place:] He saved us, not because of righteous things we had done, but because of His mercy. He saved us through the washing of rebirth and renewal by the Holy Spirit" (Titus 3:3-6).
What a glorious transformation!

This is what we must do in order to see such radical change. The same rule applies for sinner and saint. We must follow the example of David:
We must fully accept our guilt — "For I know my transgressions and my sin is always before me";
We must acknowledge that we have offended God — "Against You, You only have I sinned and done this evil in Your sight";

We must declare that God is completely blameless — "so that You are proved right when You speak and justified when You judge";

We must renounce all claims to righteousness on our own — "Surely I was sinful at birth, sinful from the time my mother conceived me";

We must commit ourselves to abandon sin and pursue the Lord — "Then will I teach transgressors Your ways, and sinners will turn back to You";

We must humble ourselves before our Maker — "The sacrifices of God are a broken spirit; a broken and contrite heart, O God, You will not despise";

We must ask for and expect mercy — this is the essence of the entire psalm!

True repentance says, "God, You are right and I am wrong. You have not failed me, I have failed You. I deserve Your judgment, and You would be completely justified in pouring out Your anger on me. But instead, in meekness and reverence, I ask You to be merciful to me, to cleanse me and make me whole, to turn my heart and renew my mind, to give me the grace to obey so that I may never go this way again — according to Your abundant kindness! Lord, I forsake my sin."

True repentance will always bear much fruit. In fact, a truly repentant person will have no objection to having his repentance tested. If he is a leader who has seriously fallen, he will gratefully submit to discipline and rehabilitation, for the truly repentant man is humble, not contentious. He is blessed just to know that he is forgiven and accepted. He will take all necessary steps to regain people's respect. He knows bearing fruit can take time.

This is how it should be with the brand new believer too. Anyone who has truly been *saved* — in the biblical sense of the word — will not continue to live the old life once he becomes aware that it is sin. He belongs to a new Master now! He will be teachable and hungry for instruction. After all, he should be joyful beyond words — if he has truly repented and become a child of the King, if he realizes that God Almighty has received him and that he has received eternal life. Salvation for the lost through repentance and faith is a quality transaction. And deliverance for the bound-up believer through repentance and faith is also a lasting event.

Unfortunately, many of God's people have failed to distinguish between repentance — a gift from God that produces lasting change — and remorse — a human feeling that never moves beyond the guilt and regret. They live in bondage for years although they "repent" dozens and dozens of times. But repentance sets the prisoners free. And "if the Son sets you free, you will be free indeed" (John 8:36).

How about you? Are you walking in freedom —
or in futility?

Chapter Twelve

It's Time to
Get Ruthless with Sin!

Sin defiles and destroys, poisons and pollutes, curses and corrupts. It is a menacing murderer and a crafty killer. It spoils everything it seduces and damns everything it dominates. *Yet we often think it is sweet.* How deceitful sin's pleasures can be. There is only one way to deal with sin and that is CUT IT OUT!

"You have heard that it was said, 'Do not commit adultery.' But I tell you that anyone who looks at a woman lustfully has already committed adultery with her in his heart. [The Lord's teaching here applies to *any outward sin* that we could also commit in our hearts.] If your right eye causes you to sin, *gouge it out and throw it away.* It is better for you to lose one part of your body that for your whole body to be thrown into hell. And if your right hand causes you to sin, *cut it off and throw it away.* It is better for you to lose one part of your body than for your whole body to go into hell" (Matt. 5:27-30).

This is how Jesus wants us to regard sin: "Would I be willing to commit this act if I knew it would cost me heaven?

Would I sin if it meant being cast into the fire of hell?" If not, then don't do it! That is the Lord's message to us. According to William Gurnall, the seventeenth century Puritan author, "The Christian is called to *proclaim and prosecute an irreconcilable war against his bosom sins*; those sins which have lain nearest his heart, must now be trampled under his feet."

God commanded Abraham to offer up his son, Isaac, his only son, whom he loved (Gen. 22:2). He commands us to do something more:

"Soul, take thy lust, thy only lust, which is the child of thy dearest love, thy Isaac, the sin which has caused most joy and laughter, from which thou hast promised thyself the greatest return of pleasure or profit; as ever thou lookest to see my face with comfort, lay hands on it and offer it up: pour out the blood of it before me; run the sacrificing knife of mortification into the very heart of it; and this freely, joyfully, for it is no pleasing sacrifice that is offered with a countenance cast down — and all this now, before thou hast one embrace more from it. Truly this is a hard chapter, flesh and blood cannot bear this saying; our lust will not lie so patiently on the altar, as Issac, or as a 'Lamb that is brought to the slaughter was dumb,' but will roar and shriek; yea, even shake and rend the heart with its hideous cries" (Gurnall).

Some of us are like the man referred to by Josh Billings "who spends half of his time in sinning and the other half in repentance." We want to change, but our willpower is weak. We resemble those who "often repent, yet never reform; [we are like] a man travelling in a dangerous path, who frequently starts and stops, but never turns back" (Bonnell Thornton). Something is wrong with our repentance!

"Now, if you find that yours is a counterfeit repentance, and you have not repented aright, mend what you have done amiss. As in the body, if a bone be set wrong, the surgeon has no way but to break it again, and set it aright; so you must do by repentance; if you have not repented aright, you must have your heart broken again in a godly manner, and be more deeply afflicted for sin than ever" (Thomas Watson).

"No man has truly repented until his sin has wounded him, until the wound has broken him and defeated him and taken all the fight and self-assurance out of him and he sees himself as the one who nailed his Saviour on the tree" (A. W. Tozer).

These are some characteristics of true repentance.

True repentance is not stopped by sympathy pains. A truly repentant woman who has been living in adultery will break free from her sinful relationship no matter how much it hurts her adulterous lover. A truly repentant cocaine addict will forsake his habit for life no matter how much his mind — and body — tell him he needs it.

True repentance is ruthless with sin and rough on the flesh. It makes the difference between grateful believers and grovelling believers, between deliverance and depression. Remorse for sins — a feeling of guilt and disgust, sometimes even with a revulsion towards the acts committed — can produce sorrow and mourning. Yet many times remorse produces worldly sorrow — a sorrow that only arises because of the ugly *consequences* of sin without ever recognizing the ugliness of sin itself — and "worldly sorrow brings death" (2 Cor. 7:10). Repentance is not just remorse!

"Never mistake remorse for repentance; remorse simply puts a man in hell while he is on earth, it carries no remedial quality with it at all, nothing that betters a man. ... Repentance is not a reaction, remorse is. Remorse is — I will never do the thing again [but it is only a temporary emotion without any power to change]. Repentance is that I deliberately become the opposite to what I have been. ... The disposition of the Son of God can only enter my life by the road to repentance" (Oswald Chambers).

True repentance goes down deep. It is *given* by God to those who have truly had it with sin, those who cannot live in it any longer. They must — absolutely, categorically and irreversibly — be free. They would rather not live at all than live an unholy life. They must be clean at any cost or any sacrifice.

Yet Satan can be so crafty! Have you ever found yourself trapped? Days, weeks or even months go by and you continue to slip and fall. Certain sins become *habitual* in your life. They seem to enslave you and pull you down. Yet you keep telling God you're sorry. You say, "Lord I want to quit!" Still, you persist in doing wrong. Nothing seems to change.

What is the problem? Many times it is *superficial repentance*. We repent superficially when at heart we have not turned from sin. We are not completely free because we don't really want to be! We still maintain the possibility of committing the same sin again (maybe if circumstances permit?). We have not truly renounced the foul habit for life. It is still too attractive to us. William Gurnall was surely right when he said: "God will never remove the guilt as long as thou entertainest the sin. ... It is desperate folly to desire God to forgive what thou intendest to commit." The Lord is looking at the heart. He is more concerned with how we respond to temptation *today* then with what we promise to do about temptation *tomorrow.*

But if we were to be completely frank, we would have to say that it is not always easy to cast sin away! Sometimes we get caught in its web. The enemy has us snared. Of course, with God, there is always a way out. Sometimes, as we "count ourselves dead to sin but alive to God in Christ" we grab hold of the reality of God's power. We throw off besetting sins like a dog shakes water off its back. Sin no longer reigns in us (Rom. 6:11-12). We are free, and free indeed! In fact, *nowhere does the Bible ever say believers should be slaves to sin.* Study it out and see for yourself. The Word is perfectly clear.

Yet some believers still find themselves enslaved — and nothing they do seems to break their chains. Paul's word to Timothy applies here:

> The Lord's servant must gently instruct those who oppose him "in the hope that God will grant them *repentance* leading them to a knowledge of the truth, and that they will come to their senses, and *escape* from the trap of the devil, who has taken them captive [literally, taken them alive] to do his will" (2 Tim. 2:24-26).

When someone's eyes are opened, when they cry out to God and mean it, when they are determined to make a change, the Lord grants them a spirit of repentance and then they too are free.

True repentance is a supernatural enabling. It produces a change of heart and causes a change in conduct. "Repentance, without amendment, is like continually pumping without mending the net" (Lorenzo Dow). That is not repentance for real. Rather, as others have said: "True repentance is to cease from sin"; "to do it no more is the truest repentance." Or in the words of another Puritan, John Trapp: "Amendment of life is the best repentance." That's why Oswald Chambers could say: "The only repentant man is the holy man, and the only holy man is the one who has been made so by the marvel of the Atonement." Repentance and holy living go hand in hand. "The best repentance is to get up and act for righteousness, and forget that you ever had relations with sin" (William James).

Some people cry and weep — yet never repent. Maybe they are upset because they got caught, or because the consequences of sin are so painful. That is not genuine repentance. In fact, as yet another godly Puritan, Thomas Watson, explains,

"Sin may be parted with yet, without repentance. 1) A man may part with some sins and keep others ... 2) An old sin may be left in order to entertain a new ... 3) A sin may be left not so much from strength of grace as from reasons of prudence. ... True leaving of sin is when the acts of sin cease from the infusion of a principle of grace, as the air ceases to be dark from the infusion of light."

The very atmosphere and climate are changed.

True repentance has a wonderful cleansing effect. One day, at the end of this age — in Israel, among the Jewish people — the Lord "will pour out on the house of David and the inhabitants of Jerusalem a spirit of grace and supplication. They will look on Me, the One they have pierced, and they will mourn for Him as one mourns for an only child, and grieve bitterly for Him as one grieves for a firstborn son" (Zech. 12:10). An overwhelming spirit of repentance will be poured out upon God's ancient people. *Then* they will recognize that the One they thought was the source of all their troubles — this One called Jesus — was actually their only source of hope. "On that day the weeping in Jerusalem will be great ..." (Zech. 12:10-14). What mourning and repentance there will be!

And the results? "On that day a fountain will be opened to the house of David and the inhabitants of Jerusalem, *to cleanse them from sin and impurity*" (Zech. 13:1). And this cleansing — the result of decades of heartbroken prayer by those who intercede for Israel — will completely transform the nation. Hallelujah! This is the day of which Isaiah spoke:

"In that day the Branch of the Lord will be beautiful and glorious [Jesus always seems especially beautiful to those who repent. After all, it is the ones who have been forgiven the most who love the most.] ... The Lord will *wash away the filth* of the women of Zion; He will *cleanse the bloodstains* from Jerusalem *by a spirit of judgment and a spirit of fire*" (Is. 4:2-4).

He will purge and purify all at once. And the people will be holy in His sight. Sin's roots will go up in smoke, and sin's stains will be washed away.

This is the essence of repentance: It produces deep-seated, lasting change. It is the key to real sanctification. It is a must for the Spirit-filled life. It sees sin for what it is and truly sorrows for sin. It not only confesses sin, but it is genuinely ashamed for sin — it hates it and turns away!

True repentance is a glorious giver of life. It is a key for a truly restored Church. But we are not yet restored. The state of our nation, the state of the world, and the state of the Body call on us to heed the exhortation of Joel:

" 'Even now,' declares the Lord, 'return to Me with all your heart, with fasting and weeping and mourning.' Rend your heart and not your garments. Return to the Lord your God, for He is gracious and compassionate, slow to anger and abounding in love, and He relents from sending

calamity. Who knows? He may turn and have pity and leave behind a blessing — grain offerings and drink offerings for the Lord your God" (Joel 2:12-14).
International repentance starts with each one of us.

Are you ready to be ruthless with sin? It is not so much the words that you speak as much as it is the attitude of your heart (great vows do not impress the Lord). Search deep and be honest with yourself. Are you flirting with lust? Are you playing games with greed? Are you letting your guard down to pride? *Pray through.* Refuse to quit. Keep the Word in front of you. Set the Lord before your eyes.

If your answer does not come today, ask, seek and knock again. *Be persistent.* You must be cleansed of the sin and the guilt. You must belong wholly to God. He will give you the power that you need. He will grant you the grace to repent. He will unlock your prison and cause you to soar — if you mean it, if you want it, if you're sincere. Leave the filthy habits at His feet for good. He will cast them far from you.

"When the soul has laid down its faults at the feet of God, it feels as though it had wings" (Eugenie de Guerin).

Are you ready to fly?

Chapter Thirteen

Jesus the King: The Center of the Kingdom of God

Today there is much talk about the kingdom of God: Is it a heavenly kingdom only? Does it include politics, education and the arts? Is it present or future or both? Is it established by man with the help of God or by God with the help of man? What exactly is the kingdom of God?

All these questions are important. Yet we may have completely missed the point. Something (or someone!) essential is often absent from the core of our kingdom preaching. In the words of William C. Burns:

> "Wherever Jesus Christ is shewn to be the Son of God with power, to be an all-sufficient Savior, a glorious Redeemer; wherever He is preached as Christ crucified, as Lord over all, as King; wherever His authority is supremely acknowledged, wherever He is adored as a Sovereign Ruler, His kingdom is preached, and men are invited to enter it."

Jesus supreme, Jesus exalted, Jesus more than all! *That is the heart of the kingdom of God.*

What is in the center of heaven itself? The throne of God Almighty. And what is in the midst of His throne? "Then I saw a Lamb, looking as if it had been slain, standing in the center of the throne, encircled by the four living creatures and the elders" (Rev. 5:6). *Everything revolves around Him*:

"The Son is the radiance of God's glory and the exact representation of His being, *sustaining all things by His powerful word*" (Heb. 1:3).

"He is before all things, *and in Him all things hold together*" (Col. 1:17).

There is nowhere higher to go.

Here is something crucial we must grasp: All of us have plans. All of us have goals. We try to fulfill the purposes of God. Yet we often find that our efforts have only served to expand *our* work, *our* influence, *our* prominence. The world has not been affected, the Church has not been built up, God's kingdom has not been advanced. But when we make it our business — our serious, earnest business — to exalt Jesus in all we say or do, then we are guaranteed success. We are cooperating with the Father. We are working with the Spirit. We are truly serving the Son.

"And He [Jesus!] is the Head of the body, the church; He is the beginning and the firstborn from among the dead, so that *in everything He might have the supremacy*. For God was pleased to have all His fullness dwell in Him" Col. 1:18-19). *That is the kingdom of God.*

Jesus was "obedient to death — even death on a cross! Therefore God exalted Him *to the highest place* and gave Him the name that is *above every name*, that at the name of Jesus *every knee should bow*, in heaven and on earth and under the earth, and *every tongue confess* that Jesus

Christ is Lord to the glory of God the Father" (Phil. 2:8-11). *That is the kingdom of God.*

Jesus the Son was raised from the dead, and God "seated Him at His right hand in the heavenly realms, *far above all rule and authority, power and dominion, and every title that can be given,* not only in the present age but also in the one to come. And God placed *all things under His feet and appointed Him to be head over everything* for the church, which is His body, the fullness of Him who fills everything in every way" (Eph. 1:20-23). *That is the kingdom of God.*

Why did the Holy Spirit come? It was to testify about Jesus, to bring glory to the Son by taking what is His and making it known to us (John 15:26, 16:14). How did the Spirit's coming affect the apostles? They spoke the Word without compromise. They preached the gospel without shame. *They lifted up Jesus without fear.* "We are witnesses of these things, and *so is the Holy Spirit* ... we cannot help speaking about what we have seen and heard" (Acts 5:32, 4:20).

How simple and powerful all this is! The Father wants His Son exalted. The Spirit has come to glorify the Lamb. He alone holds the answer for a dying world. He alone can deliver and sustain. JESUS. There is no greater name!

He must be Lord of our desires and our deeds. He must be King of our hearts and our homes. He must be Ruler of our wills and our words. *That is the kingdom of God.* We must extend His reign in all that we do — and in all that we are. With this the Father is pleased. "For the Lamb at the center of the throne will be their shepherd; He will lead them to springs of living water. And God will wipe away every tear from their eyes" (Rev. 7:17). Single-hearted devotion is the key.

Francis Frangipane recently wrote,

"Genuine love for God is an unrelenting hunger." Smith Wigglesworth carried this thought further: "To hunger and thirst after righteousness is when nothing in the world can fascinate us so much as being near to God. ... You cannot buy or wear or sell except that which is pleasing to the Lord. Jesus becomes Lord over your wants and desires. You love that which God loves and hate that which God hates. ... If you can be fascinated by anything else in the world, you don't have what God wants you to have." As Isaac Ambrose said, "Christ is never precious in man's apprehension, so long as the world seems glorious to him."

And so Samuel Rutherford cried out:

"I wish it were in my power, after this day, to [put] down [and devalue] all love but the love of Christ, and to [put] down [and devalue] all gods but Christ, all saviours but Christ, all well-beloveds but Christ, and all soul-suitors and love-beggars but Christ."

Those who love Jesus most demonstrate it by loving their spouses, children, parents, friends, co-workers — and even enemies — with gentleness and longsuffering. Putting Him first is where it all starts. Therefore "hands off, or eyes off from anything that stands in the way of Jesus Christ. ... we must not give a look, or squint at anything that may hinder this fair and lovely sight of Jesus" (Isaac Ambrose). This is devotion to our Master. This is the commitment He is due.

Do we love Him most of all? Does pleasing Him occupy the highest place in our thoughts, our ambitions, our dreams? Are we willing to lose all for the privilege of bearing His name? Then we are in harmony with God. His purpose will be accomplished through us.

Consider the small things of life. How often do we embarrass the Lord? Do our neighbors see clearly that we are followers of the Lamb? Does our day-to-day conduct — the choices we make, the way we spend our money, our behavior in times of strife — express His nature? When we get behind the wheel of our cars, does our driving magnify our Savior? If our children could not read the Word, could they learn of Jesus through us? Could we tell them, "Jesus is like me. If you've seen me then you've seen Him"? Or would we say, "Please! No! He's altogether different that what you see"?

This is where the kingdom of God is lived out. *This* is where Jesus must reign. We cannot compromise our testimonies. The world will only know Jesus through us. We are here to point people to Him — even when it hurts.

Are we willing to be cheated and wronged rather than take a fellow believer to court? This was Paul's counsel to the Corinthians! "The very fact that you have lawsuits among you means you have been completely defeated already" (1 Cor. 6:7). Are we willing to suffer quietly for *doing good* — it is no great accomplishment to suffer quietly for doing wrong — rather than violently fight for "our rights"? This was the exhortation of Peter:

"For it is commendable if a man bears up under the pain of *unjust suffering* because he is conscious of God. ... if you suffer for doing good and you endure it, this is commendable before God. To this you were called, because Christ suffered for you, leaving you an example, that you should follow in His steps" (1 Pet. 2:19-21).

When John Hyde was a missionary in India, he sometimes met people on the street wearing his own clothes. They had *stolen* them from him. But rather than accuse them or have them arrested, he simply loved them. He wanted to do nothing that would hinder his ability from sharing the gospel with them! Can we even relate to a mentality like this today? If the waitress at a restaurant is a little slow serving our table, we get grumpy and irritable. Do we care that she might watch us piously bow our heads in prayer and thank God for the food? Does our hypocrisy drive her away from the Lord? But who thinks about such things? After all, we're paying good money! We *deserve* something better than this. Actually, if we could throw out the word "deserve" and instead emphasize the word "serve" we could evangelize our country a lot more quickly.

How should we live in this world?

"Live such good lives among the pagans that, though they accuse you of doing wrong, they may see your good deeds and glorify God on the day He visits us" (1 Pet. 2:12). That is the goal of our lives — that those who were once pagans may glorify God on the day He visits us. *That is the kingdom of God.* Yet the kingdom goes deeper still.

Who is the Lord of our innermost being? Which forces dominate there? What is the state of our heart of hearts? What roots go down deep within? What kind of fruit are we bearing? We are destined to *reproduce* ourselves over and over again.

As disciples of the Lord we must be disciplined. We cannot serve one Master with our hearts and another with our appetites. *Everything* must be in submission to Him — our jobs, our money, our words; our past, our present, our future. This is what the Kingdom of God is all about. Our very personalities testify of Him. Are we refreshing or repugnant? *Jesus is reflected through us.*

"Real Christianity is marked by the pureness, the holiness, of the thoughts of man; and if the kind of Christianity you have does not produce in your mind real holiness, real purity, real sweetness, real truth, then it is a poor brand. Change it right away. ... Surely we who profess to know the living God, who profess to live in union with Him, ought to present to the world that attitude and holiness of mind which needs no recommendation. People know it; they feel it. They know it is the mind of Christ" (John G. Lake).

A kingdom is judged by the conduct of its subjects, and a king by the nature of his kingdom. We are the subjects of the heavenly kingdom. The world judges Jesus by us. He is the only true light of the world. His glory must shine forth through us. Yet we are often eclipsing the brightness of the Son of God. We are obscuring His heavenly rays. His fragrance is rarely perceived in our lives. The smell of the flesh is too strong. "One distinguishing mark of those first Christians was a supernatural radiance that shined out from within them. ... It is obvious that the average evangelical Christian today is without this radiance" (Tozer). How many radiant believers do you know — behind the pulpit *and* behind the scenes, in the work place *and* in the secret place?

We must go back to the root of all sin and reverse what has been done. We, the human race, died — as far as our true nature is concerned — when we rejected the rule of God. We are revived when we wholly submit. *The absolute and total enthroning of Jesus as Lord is the first — and last — step to restoring the glory of God.*

Listen to the message of William Chalmers Burns (March 30, 1840):
"When the kingdom of God is preached to *you*, you are invited to subject yourselves to Christ's authority, and to become faithful and devoted servants of Immanuel. ...

"You know what it is to press into any place where there is a great crowd; you do not stand listless at the door, you push your way, you press in and you enter. So it is with the kingdom of Christ; you see and feel that you must be in or you are lost, out for ever, banished to eternal darkness and torment, and therefore you press, you fight, till divine grace has subdued your proud spirit, and made you to enter into Christ's kingdom by Christ, the way, the truth, the life. ...

"He must be *all* or *nothing*: king, sovereign, ruler, governor, or absent altogether. Now, what is He to you? Is He on the throne? or only on the footstool? This is a question which may shew you whether you are really pressing in.

"Would you be contented to give up all for Christ, and take Him alone? If possessing Him were to deprive you of all you have, and all you hope for, would you bid adieu to that *all* — and to the Christian it is a *little* all — and say, 'Come, Lord Jesus, thine be the kingdom?' If not, it is because you know nothing of Christ, His character, His person, or His love. He is nothing to you. The believer, who has begun to learn the value of Christ, does not find difficulty in determining whether to give up one thing, or two things, or many things for Christ, and whether he should still be repaid for so doing. He is not always hesitating and calculating whether Christ will make up this or that loss to him. He has Christ, thrice blessed portion, and in Him, all."

That — and nothing less — is the kingdom of God.

Chapter Fourteen

All Who Have Longed for His Appearing

In one of the most moving accounts in the Bible, Jesus arrives at the village of Lazarus, and Martha, the grief stricken sister of Lazarus, greets the Lord with these words: "Lord, if You had been here, my brother would not have died" (John 11:21). Everyone was mourning and weeping. Sickness had given way to death. If only Jesus had been there! He would have healed His dear friend Lazarus. He would not have let him die. But it is four days too late and Lazarus is in the tomb. His lifeless body is already beginning to decay. It is Mary's turn to cry out: "Lord, if You had been here, my brother would not have died" (John 11:32).

Of course, we all know the rest of the story. Jesus raised Lazarus from the dead! But that is not what I want to emphasize here. That is not the burden of my heart. What is burning so strongly within me is something else entirely. *If Jesus were only here* — in our services, in our homes, in our hearts, *in this world* — things would be so much different! There would not be so many others like Lazarus, cut down before their time — and never raised from the dead. There would not be so many shattered lives, crushed by the weight of suffering — who never experience relief. There would not be so many unanswered cries for deliverance — if only Jesus were here! Do we really believe that if the Lord attended our meetings — I mean *literally* attended our meetings, actually walking down the aisles, touching the sick and afflicted, sharing His heart with the lost — that we would still see the same paltry results? "Lord, if You were only here, things would be so much different!" Obviously, something is getting in the way. His Spirit's presence is being obstructed.

But the problem goes beyond our own limited needs. What about the rest of the world? *The suffering of mankind is beyond measure.* Consider the pain that grips this fallen world: Who will make Cambodia whole after *half of its population* was slaughtered and starved to death? Who will restore the Jewish people, after *six million* of their own brothers and sisters — two-thirds of the entire European community — were systematically annihilated in cold blood? Who will stand up for the families of the *multiplied millions* of Russians who were victims of Stalin's fiendish purges? And today, who will help the countless refugees, the innumerable starving children, the miserably poor and oppressed? Who will replace the thousands of teenage boys who were mowed down in senseless battles between Iran and Iraq? Who will mend the fracture of the African nations so ravaged by rebel war — Mozambique, Liberia, Angola, Ethiopia — all with stories too brutal to tell? Who will heal this human race, a race so riddled with disease, corruption and death?

Is a new evangelistic program or another prayer meeting or more church planting the answer? The thought seems absurd. The needs of mankind are too staggering. Our best efforts fall tragically short. We are giving aspirin to a dying man. We barely touch the source of human pain!

How can this broken world be restored? Who can bind up its wounds? There is one answer, and one answer alone. Sooner or later, all of us will have to accept it. *The only hope for mankind, the only salvation for this planet, is the return of the Son of God.* Until then, suffering and death will continue. Until then, tragedy will be the way of life for untold millions. Until then, the wail of the bereaved will be heard. If only Jesus were here!

Of course, until that day comes, we *must* reach out. We *must* relieve hunger and heartache — one hurting person at a time. Every life is important to God. Each one counts before Him. But in the midst of all of our activity, we must never lose sight of the overall cure: "Maranatha! O Lord, come!" *That* must be the ultimate goal of our ministry. As we go and make disciples of the nations, we hasten the Lord's return. "And this gospel of the kingdom will be preached in the whole world as a testimony to all nations, and then the end will come" (Matt. 24:14). Jesus will heal the nations. Let us help draw redemption near.

As Paul approached the close of his earthly life, he shared his heart with Timothy:
    "I have fought the good fight, I have finished the race, I have kept the faith. Now there is in store for me the crown of righteousness, which the Lord, the righteous Judge, will award to me on that day — and not only to me, but also to all who have longed for His appearing" (2 Tim. 4:7-8).
All who have longed for His appearing — they will receive the crown. Their hearts have cried out, "Lord, come quickly!"; their sobs have rent the heavens, "Lord, how long?";

their souls have yearned for that day when sorrow shall be no more! "Lord Jesus, how we long for Your appearing!" *The whole earth will be changed.*

Paul's words are so profound and deep. The return of Jesus is not just an event on God's "end-time prophetic calendar." It is not just the time for us to meet Him in the clouds. *It is the time of deliverance for the world.* It is the time of restoration. Until then we must mourn and weep — and God will take note of our tears.

"The Israelites groaned in their slavery and cried out, and their cry for help because of their slavery went up to God. God heard their groaning and He remembered His covenant with Abraham, with Isaac and with Jacob. So God looked on the Israelites and was concerned about them" (Ex. 2:23-25).

"And will not God bring about justice for His chosen ones, who cry out to Him day and night? Will He keep putting them off? I tell you, He will see that they get justice, and quickly" (Luke 18:7-8).

Many centuries ago, when the priests of Israel were corrupt and godlessness was the predominant way of life, Malachi wrote:

"Then those who feared the Lord talked with each other, and the Lord listened and heard. A scroll of remembrance was written in His presence concerning those who feared the Lord and honored His name. 'They will be Mine,' says the Lord Almighty, 'in the day when I make up My treasured possession' " (Mal. 3:16-17). They were grieved by the sins of God's people, so the Lord was pleased to call them His own.

In Ezekiel's day, as Jerusalem was about to be judged by Babylon, the prophet had a vision. He saw six men approaching, each one armed with weapons of destruction. They were given a hard commission: "Kill off graybeard, youth and maiden, women and children; but do not touch any person who bears the mark. Begin here at My Sanctuary" (Ezek. 9:6, NJV). Who were those who bore the mark? "Pass through the city, through Jerusalem, and *put a mark on the foreheads of the men who groan and moan because of all the abominations that are committed in it*" (Ezek. 9:4, NJV). Those are the ones God will honor on that day. They have already been singled out. *Those who bear His mark today will wear His crown tomorrow.*

What is God's Word to those who are not just burdened because of the sufferings of others, but are going through great trials themselves? The answer for them is the same: Jesus will come back! Then all suffering will cease.

The Thessalonians were experiencing great persecution and hardship, but Paul encouraged them to look ahead. The day would come when the Lord Jesus would be "revealed from heaven in blazing fire with His powerful angels." He will "give relief to you who are troubled, and to us as well ... [when] He comes to be glorified in His holy people and to be marveled at among all those who have believed" (2 Thess. 1:5-10). What an event that will be! *Trouble will be gone forever.*

And so Peter and James encouraged the persecuted disciples to eagerly await Jesus' arrival:
"Dear friends, do not be surprised at the painful trial you are suffering, as though something strange happened to you. But rejoice that you participate in the sufferings of Christ, so that you may be overjoyed *when His glory is revealed*" (1 Pet. 4:12-13).
Our trials will have an end! "Be patient, then, brothers, until the Lord's coming. ... be patient and stand firm, because the

Lord's coming is near" (James 5:7-8). Hold out and endure until then. Wait for the Lord to intervene. Messiah will return!

When Jesus comes back:
    Zion will be renewed with shouts of joy, and sorrow and sighing will flee;
    Violence and terror will be over, and senseless atrocities will cease;
    Our mortal bodies will be transformed, and disease will die for good;
    The groaning of all creation will end, "and the lion will eat straw like the ox. ... They will neither harm nor destroy on all my holy mountain, for the earth will be full of the knowledge of the Lord as the waters cover the sea" (Is. 11:7,9).
Paradise will truly be restored!

On that day the people of God will be in perfect unity. No more deception, no more dissension, no more strife, no more sin, no more factions, no more failures, no more complaints, no more compromise! "Oh Lord, we want You to come!"

On that day disappointment will cease. No more funeral services, no more widows and orphans, no more wheelchairs, no more hospitals, no more birth defects, no more handicapped children — not even family pets run over by the side of the road! "Jesus, if only You were here!"

"O when will we meet! O how long is it to the dawning of the marriage day! O sweet Jesus, take wide steps! O my Lord, come over mountains at one stride! O my Beloved, flee as a roe or young hart upon the mountains of separation" (Samuel Rutherford). "Jesus, we long for Your return!"

How can we bring Him back?

"Since everything will be destroyed in this way [the universe will be renovated by fire], what kind of people ought you to be? You ought to live holy and godly lives as you look forward to the day of God *and speed its coming*" (2 Pet. 3:11-12).

What a scandal that we do not look forward to the day of God! What a shame that we do not long for the Lord's return! How perverse that we do not always cry out, "Heavenly Father, Your kingdom come!" How incomprehensible that we do not live our lives with a deep desire to see Jesus come back!

Could it be that we are at home in this world? Could it be that we feel too cozy down here? Many of us would have to admit that we are content with things as they are. How can we change our hearts? Visit a children's hospital; spend a day by a funeral parlor; read the tragic stories in today's latest news; talk to maimed veterans from Vietnam; meet the disfigured patients of a burn clinic in their agony. And then, as if the human soul could even contemplate any more grief, think of all the horrible crimes committed every hour by man against man — the murders, the abuse, the torture. How comfortable are you now? If only Jesus were here! Isn't the pain overwhelming? How we need the Lord to appear!

BUT HE WILL COME AGAIN! As surely as He came and raised up Lazarus, He will come and raise us up.

"The body that is sown is perishable, it is raised imperishable; it is sown in dishonor, it is raised in glory; it is sown in weakness, it is raised in power; it is sown a natural body, it is raised a spiritual body. ... We will not all sleep, but we will all be changed — in a flash, in the twinkling of an eye, at the last trumpet. For the trumpet will sound, the dead will be raised imperishable, and we will be changed " (1 Cor. 15:42-44,51-53).

Hallelujah! He who is the Resurrection and the Life will return. HE WILL COME AGAIN!

" 'Men of Galilee,' [the angels] said, 'why do you stand here looking into the sky? This same Jesus, who has been taken from you into heaven, will come back in the same way you have seen Him go into heaven' " (Acts 1:11). As surely as He ascended from the earth 2,000 years ago, He will descend from the heavens at the end of this age. "For the Son of Man is going to come in His Father's glory with His angels, and then He will reward each person according to what he has done" (Matt. 16:27). These are the words of Jesus, the One who cannot lie!

"Behold, I am coming soon!
Blessed is he who keeps the words of
the prophecy in this book" (Rev. 22:7).

"Behold, I am coming soon!
My reward is with Me, and I will give to everyone
according to what he has done" (Rev. 22:12).

"He who testifies to these things says,
'Yes, I am coming soon.' Amen. Come, Lord Jesus"
(Rev. 22:20).

AMEN! JESUS, COME!

Chapter Fifteen
The Samson Cycle

Samson is one of the most tragic figures in the Bible. He had so much given to him, such an awesome anointing and call. But he went the way of the flesh and the world. Ultimately it cost him both his eyes and his life.

He was a loose-living "man of God." He would have his fling and then settle back down. He would fight with the Philistine men and sleep with the Philistine women. He fell right into the enemy's trap. He who had been so invincible, he who caused his foes to tremble, became captive to unbridled lust. Delilah became his wife.

Three times this beautiful, treacherous woman sought to discover the secret of his strength. Three times he misled her. But the fourth time he gave in and told her all his heart:
" 'No razor has ever been used on my head,' he said, 'because I have been a Nazirite set apart to God since birth. If my head were shaved, my strength would leave me, and I would become as weak as any other man' " (Judg. 16:17). While he slept in Delilah's lap, his long locks were shaved off. *But he had no idea what she was doing.*

The Philistines entered the room, and Delilah called out, " 'Samson, the Philistines are upon you!' He awoke from his sleep and thought, 'I'll go out as before and shake myself free.' *But he did not know that the Lord had left him"* (Judg. 16:20). Immediately his enemies seized him, gouged out his eyes, bound him with bronze shackles, and sent him to do humiliating work in the prison. What a pitiful, lamentable scene! But as he worked those degrading hours of slave labor, his hair began to grow back (Judg. 16:21-22). His miserable state became the key to his deliverance.

This applies to the Charismatic Church!

Like Samson, we were given a special anointing and call, a great commission to bring spiritual restoration. Like Samson, we were Nazirites in our earliest years, truly set apart from this world to the Lord. And like Samson, we have been seduced by the lusts of the flesh. We have lost our true strength while sleeping on Delilah's lap. We have broken our holy covenant with God. *And like Samson, we don't even know that His presence has greatly left us.*

This is where we stand today: Our enemies are rising against us. They taunt and mock and accuse. But we have no fear at all. We are the Spirit-filled ones. We are the anointed of God. We will drive off our foes. Instead, we are in for an ugly surprise. Our enemies are about to humiliate us before the world. (Actually the humiliation has already begun!) They are about to bring us down from our proud, lofty heights. *We have lost the real source of our power.* Yet we think that we are so strong!

Like Samson, we have made many mistakes along the way — yet somehow God has preserved us. Like Samson, we have flirted with sin — yet it has not cost us everything so far! But like Samson, we think we will awake from our sleep; we think we will "go out as before and shake ourselves free" — but this time it will not work. *In ourselves we cannot win.*

For years Samson walked in a mighty anointing — tearing apart lions, killing the enemies of Israel, displaying the great power of God. But eventually the flesh caught up with him and he reaped the awful harvest he had sown. Sin — not the Philistines, not Delilah, not the devil — became his undoing. It will be our undoing too.

For years we have been able to live as we please — so little discipline, so lax in holiness, so lacking in integrity — yet the Lord has not left us ... *or so we think.* Whenever our enemies have come upon us, we have been able to fight them away. But while we have been sleeping — congratulating ourselves at our endless conferences, always boasting of our great deeds, hardly realizing that danger is at the door — the world has cut off our hair. *Our disloyalty has finally caught up with us.* Unless a massive wave of revival sweeps through our land, there can be only one way to victory from here.

Like Samson, we must be brought down. In the world's eyes it will be our defeat. We will be humbled before our enemies — our empires collapsing, our leaders exposed, our big men falling to the ground. And the world will have its time to mock: "Our god has delivered our enemy into our hands, the one who laid waste our land and multiplied our slain" (Judg. 16:24).

Disorientation will quickly set in. Our vision and purpose will be lost. As we seem to be prisoners bound up in chains, these questions will dominate our minds: "How could we have thought that *we* were the ones who were going to shake the nations, that *we* were the answer for a dying world, that *we* had the authority and might? How could we have been so blind when we were so sure we had clear sight?"

Then the revelation will come: We really had no might of our own. Our efforts couldn't have saved even a fly. Our finest campaigns, our biggest media blitzes, all our books and tapes and shows were only tools in the hands of the Lord. *He* is the strength of our life. At that time — and not before — in our lowly and humble estate, we will suddenly realize that something is happening. Our hair is beginning to grow back.

Like Samson we will be led into the stronghold of those who hate us. We will be expected to perform for their jeers. But the anointing of God will be with us. His presence will have returned! And as we pray a new kind of prayer — a prayer of total dependence, a prayer of holy anger against the enemy of our souls, a prayer that does not care for this world — *the fortress of Satan will crumble.* Great victory will explode on this world!

"So they called Samson out of the prison, and he performed for them. When they stood him among the pillars [the temple was crowded with men and women, with about three thousand on the roof], Samson said to the servant who held his hand, 'Put me where I can feel the pillars that support the temple, so that I may lean against them.' ... Then Samson prayed to the Lord, 'O Sovereign Lord, remember me. O God, please strengthen me just once more, and let me with one blow get revenge on the Philistines for my two eyes.' Then Samson reached toward the two central pillars on which the temple stood. Bracing himself against them, his right hand on the one and his left hand on the other, Samson said, 'Let me die with the Philistines!' Then he pushed with all his might, and down came the temple on the rulers and all the people in it. *Thus he killed many more when he died than while he lived"* (Judg. 16:25-30).

This speaks so forcefully to us! We will accomplish far more for the kingdom of God — and wreak more havoc on the kingdom of darkness — in our death than in our life. We have become so self-confident, so self-sufficient, so self-assured. *But all this is coming to an end.* We have cut ourselves off from the resources of our God. He will cut off His blessing from us until we learn to cry out again, "Lord, remember us this one time!" How desperately we need the Lord!

We cannot even pretend to lift a finger without Him. We have no power, no dominion of our own. His Spirit is our strength, His Word is our food, His Son is our light and our life. We are dull without Him, aimless and lost. We must be driven back by the way of the cross. That alone has been — and always will be — the sole source of our salvation.

Enough with our emphasis on talents and abilities. Enough with our emphasis on anointing and gifts. There is one thing that really matters for the servant of God. What is the condition of his heart?

"How diligently the cavalry officer keeps his sabre clean and sharp; every stain he rubs off with the greatest care. Remember you are God's servant — His instrument — I trust a chosen vessel unto Him to bear His name. In great measure, according to the purity and perfections of the instrument, will be the success. *It is not great talents God blesses so much as great likeness to Jesus.* A holy minister is an awful weapon in the hand of God" (Robert Murray M'Cheyne, writing to Rev. Daniel Webster).

If Samson had stayed humble, if he had not played games with the enemy, if he had walked carefully before the Lord, he would never have been brought so low. But his loose living dragged him down. Lust tore his very eyes out. (It will torment and blind us too.) Samson could have been so greatly used. He could have been a mighty deliverer. He could have brought much glory to God. Instead his name evokes pain. Oh, Samson, how different things could have been ...

Is the Charismatic Church a modern-day Samson? Let us examine our souls before God. He knows the real heart of our leaders. He knows how much complacency has crept in. He knows how low we must go — until we come to the very end of ourselves. This much is sure: For the Charismatic Church, just like Samson ...

the way to restoration is humiliation

and the way to victory is death.

Chapter Sixteen

The Power of Consecration to Principle

In October of 1977, in three prison cells in Germany, a suicide pact was carried out. Three terrorists, leaders of the notorious Baader-Meinhoff gang, exchanged secret communications. They agreed to take their own lives at a specified time. In spite of the tightest security, they ingeniously devised mechanisms for self-murder — and suddenly they were gone.

The international press reported the news. Their deaths were the talk of the hour. But their triple suicide was more than just another grisly story. It was orchestrated to carry a clear message, to broadcast a strong signal to their colleagues who had just suffered defeat in another land: "We have sealed our mission with our lives. You go and do the same. Take courage and fight to the death. We have given you a beacon of hope." All this for the kingdom of hell!

Then there were the self-proclaimed "soldiers" from the Irish Republic Army, literally starving themselves to death in British prison cells because they believed they had to stand up for their "rights." They withered away to nothing and passed from this world for good — for their vision, their dream, their goal. And it was not a dream given by God! Yet they perished for it just the same.

Fanaticism, you say? I disagree. It was total consecration to a *wrong* principle, complete dedication to a *misguided* vision. It was the conviction to die for the very things they lived for — even though what they lived for was fatally wrong. These men and women, so deceived by the enemy and so destroyed by his cunning, did what was only logical. They gave themselves wholly for what was dear to them: their call and their cause. What they did was consistent and clear. In a perverted way it even made sense.

What does *not* make sense is this: We who call ourselves children of the one true God, who believe that we have been ransomed from a dark eternity, who proclaim that we are living at the tail end of this age, who speak of cosmic warfare between the forces of heaven and hell — *we* live flabby, undisciplined, unconsecrated, spineless lives. What has become of courage? Where has conviction gone? Where are the *heroes* of the faith — the brave pioneers and patriots of our day? Where are those driven by a spirit of discovery and advance for the kingdom of our Lord?

Consider the early history of our nation (remember, we had to fight a bloody war of independence). People died for this country, for what it could be — something unique, something new, something truly free. There was Nathan Hale, the daring spy caught behind enemy lines and hung the next day without trial. His last words are a powerful testimony to what it means to *give* yourself to a cause: "I only regret that I have but one life to lose for my country." He gladly would have done it again!

And then there was the battle cry for freedom sounded by Patrick Henry, the brilliant lawyer and orator, taking a firm public stand with no hope of turning back: "I know not what course others may take; but as for me, give me liberty or give me death!" And he wasn't even thinking of the age to come. He meant liberty in this life, in this present world — for himself, for his family, for his people. It was important enough to live for. It was important enough to die for.

This has been the driving force behind martyrs and missionaries, pioneers and patriots through the ages: the power of consecration to principle and the willingness to sacrifice, strive, suffer and even die for a cause. It is something sadly lacking among us today. *We are spoiled.* Let the truth be told!

"Believe me, it is not with folded hands and drowsy consciences, and hearts full of the cares of this life, but denying ourselves, taking up the cross, bearing the reproach, and by following the Lamb whithersoever He goeth, that we shall enter the kingdom" (William C. Burns).

We need more men in our generation like David Brainerd. He pushed his frail dying body mile after mile, heaving and coughing and spitting up blood, drenched by the thunderstorms as he rode his horse by day, and soaked by his feverish sweat as he slept in the wild by night. But there were more American Indians to be reached. So onward and onward he went — bemoaning his lack of zeal all the way!

We need more women today like Gladys Aylward, the British housemaid who gave her life for China. Rejected for service by the board of the China Inland Mission because of a serious learning disability, she saved her pennies and at the age of twenty-eight packed two suitcases, a bedroll, "a bag clanking with a small stove and pots and pans," and set out for her goal — by train, through Europe, Russia and Siberia. Unfortunately, she was heading straight into a border dispute between Russia and China, entering a literal war zone. The train she was aboard, filled with Russian soldiers, suddenly stopped amid the sound of distant gun fire. She was told she had to get out. The ride was over!

Alone in Siberia — a single woman in a totally strange land in the middle of winter — she began the long walk back to the nearest city:

    " 'The Siberian wind blew the powdered snow around her heels, and she carried a suitcase in each hand, one still decorated ludicrously with kettle and saucepan. Around her shoulders she wore [her] fur rug.' By dawn, after having taken a two-hour rest next to her little alcohol stove, she could see the lights of Chita in the distance" (Ruth Tucker, quoting Alan Burgess).

Undaunted, she continued on her way, having to go through Manchuria and then Japan to reach her destination.

This single woman, who even doubted she was God's first choice for the job ("There was somebody else. ... I don't know who it was — God's first choice. It must have been a man — a wonderful man. A well-educated man. I don't know what happened. Perhaps he died. Perhaps he wasn't willing. ... And God looked down ... and saw Gladys Aylward"), this courageous soul actually moved behind enemy lines during Japan's bombing of China, ministering to the needs of the villagers, and supernaturally protecting her "family" of nearly one hundred adopted children. God grant us noble hearts like hers!

We need more heroic evangelists in our land, the John Wesley's of today.

"In February of 1745 he left London with Richard Moss, one of his converts ... They rode first through mire and water, and then over snow and ice. The last stage was the worst, as a hard frost, on top of a partial thaw, had made all the ground like glass. Then the snow began to fall again and [the entire place] 'appeared a great pathless waste of white.' Even though they knew the area, they were at a loss to find the way to [their destination] until someone guided them in. They had covered 280 miles in six days — averaging close on fifty miles a day in extreme conditions. 'Many a rough journey have I had before,' Wesley wrote afterwards, 'but one like this I never had; between wind, and hail, and rain, and ice, and snow, and driving sleet, and piercing cold. But it is past: those days will return no more, and are therefore, as though they had never been' " (A. Skevington Wood).
Of course, there had been no thought of turning back. This was the Master's business!

We need more of the courageous missionary spirit in our midst that will die before it will quit. When financial support had been cut off for John Lake's workers in South Africa, he gathered them all together from throughout the land. He informed them that there was no money for now — and he had no guarantee of funds for tomorrow. One day, after meeting for a few minutes alone, these dedicated men invited Lake to return to the room, which they had just rearranged for a communion service. They had made a solemn determination:

"Brother Lake, [they said,] during your absence we have come to a conclusion; we have made our decision. We want you to serve the Lord's supper. We are going back to our fields. We are going back if we have to walk back. We are going back if we have to starve. We are going back if our wives die. We are going back if our children die. We are going back if we die ourselves. We have but one request. If we die, we want you to come and bury us."

That next year, in Lake's own moving words,

"I buried twelve men, sixteen wives and children. In my judgment, if they had a few of the things a white man needs to eat, but what they might have lived. Friends, when you want to find out why the power of God came down from heaven in South Africa like it never came before since the days of the apostles, there is your answer."

Jesus spoke of "My blood" in the New Testament communion cup, and then said to His disciples, *"All of you* drink of it." This, to Lake, meant:

"Let us become one. Let us become one in our purpose to die for the world. Your blood and Mine, together. 'My blood in the New Testament.' It is My demand for you. It is your high privilege."

"Friends, [Lake continued,] the group of missionaries that followed me went without food, and went without clothes, and once when one of my preachers was sunstruck, and had wandered away, I tracked him by the blood marks on his feet. ... That is the kind of consecration that established Pentecost in South Africa [today there are more than *one-half million* believers in the churches that had their origins in Lake's *five year* ministry there at the turn of this century]. ... That is the kind of consecration that will get answers from heaven. That is the kind God will honor. That is the consecration to which I would pledge Pentecost. ... Ye who are ready to die for Christ and this glorious Pentecostal Gospel, we salute you. You are brothers with us and with your Lord."

This was the heart of Paul:

"I eagerly expect and hope that I will in no way be ashamed, but will have *sufficient courage* so that now as always Christ will be exalted in my body, whether by life or by death. For to me, to live is Christ and to die is gain" (Phil. 1:20-21).

He had lost his life in the cause of his Lord.

This was the secret strength that enabled righteous martyrs like Ignatius to say,

"Now at last I begin to be a disciple! ... Come fire, come cross, come whole herds of wild beasts, come drawing and quartering, scattering of bones, crushing of the whole body, all the horrible blows of the devil — let all these things come upon me, if only I may be with Christ."

Yet he was a mortal just like us! Can we relate to such a spirit today? "I am the wheat of God," Ignatius wrote as he was being brought to Rome for his martyrdom, "and am ground by the teeth of the wild beasts, that I may be found the pure bread of God."

More than 400 years ago, as the flames began to jump at the feet of the Protestant martyr Dr. Nicholas Ridley, his colleague, Bishop Hugh Latimer — who in a moment would be burned alive too — cried out to him and said, "Be of good comfort, Master Ridley, and play the man. We shall this day light such a candle, by God's grace, in England, as I trust shall never be put out." Human torches for the kingdom of God!

Look at *your* hands, *your* feet, *your* body, *your* blood. Picture giving *yourself* — your flesh and bones — to be torn apart by starving animals, or to be eaten up by fire while you stand chained to the stake — all because you confess the Lord Jesus! And remember — you do all this entirely *by choice*. You *lay your life down* for your Master.

Or think back to the very sickest day you ever experienced — before any healing came. Remember the pain, the nausea, the weakness, and then imagine dragging yourself out of bed, walking all day and all night in biting cold and beating rain — just to tell some lost souls about the Savior. Picture doing it all on your own, all alone, yet willingly, joyfully for the glory of the Lord. *Jesus did it for us.* He is the Pioneer and Pathfinder of our faith. He calls us to walk as He did.

Several years ago a Christian man living in the oppressive country of Albania found some gospel literature that had floated ashore. It was secretly sent in by workers from the Christian Mission to the Communist World, since there were hardly any other ways to get Bibles and tracts into that land. This brother found more and more literature and began to distribute it among his people.

"For his small missionary work, our Albanian brother was put in a dark prison and tortured, [relates Richard Wurmbrand, the director of the Christian Mission.] He showed our workers the scars on his wrists from the screws that were tightened almost beyond endurance. The pain was maddening. Then he was cut with knives and burned with red-hot iron pokers. The marks were visible on his abdomen.

"Our worker, Bro. Symanck, asked, 'Are you angry at us for an activity that sent you to jail?' He replied, 'No. I am happy, because it was worthwhile. Such writings deserve our sacrifices for their distribution.' " Can we say anything less?

Let us have the "Abraham kind of faith" that "looked forward to the city with foundations, whose architect and builder is God" (Heb. 11:10). We are pilgrims and aliens too, marching towards our heavenly goal. Let us set our sights as Moses did: "He chose to be mistreated along with the people of God rather than enjoy the pleasures of sin for a short time. He regarded disgrace for the sake of Christ as of greater value than the treasures of Egypt, because he was looking ahead to his reward" (Heb. 11:24-25).

Egypt's riches are all around us as well. We must focus on Him who is invisible. This is the call of *every* believer. It is essential; it is basic; it must be.

Of course, not all of us are called to leave houses and families, careers and educations, to trek off to some distant land. *But all of us are called to breathe that very same spirit of absolute consecration, courage and commitment to the kingdom of God*: Parents taking an unshakable stand for true holiness in the home. ... Young people preaching boldly on the streets of our fallen cities. ... Businessmen of real integrity willing to suffer major losses rather than compromise. ... Pastors with eyes fixed on heaven living selflessly for their flocks. ... Godly missionaries raising high the banner of Jesus in a hostile land. ... Disciplined prayer warriors interceding for the dying with broken hearts. ... Zealous believers dissolving their assets to give their all for the poor. ... Blood-washed saints clothed with righteousness as the very fabric and essence of their lives. ... The Church of Jesus refusing to yield even one square inch of territory to the devil. This is what it will take if we want to see the true restoration of the glory of God.

Something that precious will not come cheap.

Chapter Seventeen

Entering the Most Holy Place

God is strikingly holy — overwhelmingly, awesomely, inexpressibly holy. He is completely separate and other — absolutely free from sin and evil, totally good and pure. He is perfect light, perfect truth, perfect justice and perfect love. There is nothing to fully compare Him to; there are no words that adequately describe Him. He cannot be explained, only exalted; He cannot be analyzed, only adored. He is not just holy, but "Holy, holy, holy." What else can we say? Seeing His splendor is more than we can bear. Beholding His presence is completely overpowering.

Moses could not approach the burning bush. He had to remove the sandals from his feet. *The very ground had become holy.* The Israelites could not come near Mount Sinai. They had to wash their clothes and abstain from relations with their wives. Their normal habits had to be adjusted. Almighty God was about to appear. *And He is exactly the same today.* He is not one degree less holy. His nature has not changed at all. He calls *us* to draw near. He calls us to be *like Him.* What a staggering thought. Could anything be more impossible unless He intervened?

This is something we must understand: *The blood of Jesus does not reduce the holiness of God one bit.* Instead — incredibly, miraculously — it gives us access into His throne room. The all-holy dwelling place of the all-holy Lord is now accessible to us. But we must come with awe, wonder and respect. Heaven forbid that we treat this lightly!

Yet this is exactly what we have done. Our prayers often border on crass familiarity; our choruses often sound like jingles. Our preaching is not calculated to produce *godly* fear; our "ministry in the gifts" inspires little reverence. *It is crucial that we recover the holiness of God.* There is no seeing His glory without it.

Let's look back to the Law. Immediately some things become clear. God's holiness is concrete. He is literally set apart and distinguished from "the world" — from all that is unclean and corrupt. Those who approach Him must be the same — separated from that which defiles and separated to that which is pure. That is the meaning of *holy* — set apart for the service of God. Only unblemished offerings could be brought before Him — after all, He was the holy God. Nothing else would be fitting. In fact, anything else would be insulting:

" 'When you bring injured, crippled or diseased animals and offer them as sacrifices, should I accept them from your hands?' says the Lord. ... 'For I am a great king,' says the Lord Almighty, 'and My name is to be feared among the nations' " (Mal. 1:13-14).

Only "unblemished" priests could serve Him. Among Aaron's descendants, no man with *any defect* — being blind, lame, disfigured or deformed, having a crippled foot or hand, being hunchbacked or dwarfed, having any eye defect, festering or running sores, or damaged testicles — "no descendant of Aaron the priest who has any defect is to come near to present the offerings made to the Lord by fire" (Lev. 21:16-21). This is awfully exacting, and it applies in the spirit to us! Willful, habitual defects in our inner-beings — lusts, corruptions, pollutions of any kind — disqualify us from approaching the Lord in service.

First we must come for cleansing by the power of the blood of the Lamb. We cannot treat this lightly. Being a priest is quite a high call. We must once and for all give up our disgraceful outward shows — dancing, clapping, raising our hands to the Lord in the public assembly, offering up our sacrifices of praise — if our lives are filled with uncleanness and riddled with disobedience and flesh. Let's be priests who truly minister to the Lord, not priests who tritely mock Him.

We must also get rid of all hyper-spiritual notions that make God's holiness theological or abstract. His holiness is as real as the food the Israelites ate and as tangible as the clothes they wore. It dictated the way the women lived after childbirth and the way the men conducted themselves when they went out to war. A holy God dwelt in their midst. Wrong behavior could drive Him away.

"You are the children of the Lord your God. Do not cut yourselves or shave the front of your heads for the dead, for you are people holy to the Lord your God. Out of all the peoples on the face of the earth, the Lord has chosen you to be His treasured possession. ... Do not eat anything you find already dead. ... [For] you are a people holy to the Lord your God" (Deut. 14:1-2,21). Carcasses are not for you!

"The Lord said to Moses, 'Speak to the entire assembly of Israel and say to them: "Be holy because I, the Lord your God, am holy. Each of you must respect his mother and father, and you must observe My Sabbaths. ... Do not turn to idols or make gods of cast metal for yourselves. ... Do not steal. Do not lie. Do not deceive one another. ... Do not mate different kinds of animals. Do not plant your fields with two kinds of seeds. Do not wear clothing woven of two kinds of material" ' " (Lev. 19:1-4,11,19).
God despises all foreign mixtures — just like He despises dishonoring of parents, worshipping of idols, stealing, lying or deceiving. This is a message for us as well. Let us ask the Holy Spirit for light.

"When you are encamped against your enemies ... designate a place outside the camp where you can go to relieve yourself. As part of your equipment have something to dig with, and when you relieve yourself, dig a hole and cover up your excrement. *For the Lord your God moves about in your camp* to protect you and to deliver your enemies to you. *Your camp must be holy,* so that He will not see among you anything indecent and turn away from you" (Deut. 23:9,12-14).

Are you starting to get the picture? Holiness is not *religious.* It reflects the very nature of the Creator and King and it involves every single area of our lives. Murder, adultery, greed, theft, irreverence, slander, immodesty, uncleanness, selfishness, hatred — SINS of all kinds — drive His holy presence away. How could He possibly tabernacle in the midst of such ungodly filth? How could He answer some of us when we lift our voices and pray, "Take me past the outer court into the holy place"?

Actually, it's a wonder that we can even sing that beautiful song without breaking into a cold sweat. What are we really thinking when we cry out, "Take me past the brazen altar, Lord, *I want to see Your face*?" Do we have any conception of what we are asking for when we say, "Take the coal, *cleanse my lips*" — lips that barely ten minutes ago were gossiping, lips that only yesterday were speaking harshly to the children, lips that sound so pious on the outside but cover up a heart of sin. "Take the coals, touch *my* lips, here I am." My Lord and my God, be merciful!

Over and over in Leviticus and Numbers, God gave specific laws to the priests and the Levites. He carefully laid out what they could and could not do — "so that you will not die." If they violated His holiness they were gone. That's why Uzzah was struck dead on the spot when he stretched forth his hand to steady the ark, God's ark, which was not to be touched. No human hands could tamper with it. *The ark was where THE LORD appeared.* And now His ark dwells in our midst. "Handle with care!" He says.

God told Aaron and his sons that they had to "distinguish between the holy and the common, between the unclean and the clean" (Lev. 10:10). Unfortunately, many believers over the years have gotten caught up in legalistic holiness, emphasizing outward forms and external norms. This has turned many away from the truth. But there *are* eternal standards of God; there *are* things clean and unclean. We must learn to distinguish and discern, lest we ignore the words of the Law. There *are* abominations in God's sight. There *are* certain things that He hates. If it was wrong for the Canaanites, it's wrong for us. (Let's not even worry right now about what was wrong for *Israel.* If the Church put away all the sins of the *pagans,* that would be a big step forward.)

In Leviticus, chapter 18, the Lord stated that He expelled the Canaanites from the land because of incest, homosexuality, bestiality, sacrificing their children to Molech, and having intercourse with their wives during their periods. All this was detestable in His sight. What makes it any less detestable today? It still matters to the Lord. (Please don't get angry with me if you disagree with this. I'm only telling you what the Word says. Take it up with the Author!)

There is a major lesson we must learn. We want a 100% restoration of the power and gifts of the Spirit, even though we may only be 25% restored when it comes to morality, personal holiness, family life, church structure, doctrine and practice. It simply will not happen this way! The vessels are not ready and the stage has not been set. I can almost hear God say again, "You are a stiff-necked people. If I were to go with you even for a moment, I might destroy you. Now take off your ornaments and I will decide what to do with you" (Ex. 33:5). The Church of the Lord must come clean!

Ignorance is no excuse (remember the Laodiceans!). We need the blinders removed. We parade around beaches indecently exposed (no one can tell me that today's bathing suits are not unclean and defiling); we enter church buildings in lustful display (no one can justify wearing sensually suggestive, clinging, revealing outfits); we actually *pay* for all kinds of smut to be brought into our homes (don't even *think* of trying to defend this). We are plagued by divorce and affairs (really, things in the Church weren't always that bad!); we don't properly train our children in the way they should go (disrespect and disdain for parental authority used to be the exception, not the rule); we are dominated by the gods of materialism and greed (yes, idolatry is still rampant today). This list only scratches the surface.

Although we are called by God to reach out to the poor and minister to the sick and afflicted, most of us have never prayerfully *read* Luke 14:12-14, let alone obeyed God and done it. Although we are called to be one in the Lord and live united in heart and in mind, each day the Church experiences new division and even small congregations split. Although we are called to make disciples of the nations of the world and to win them before they are lost, we are steadily falling behind, since far more people are being born than being born again. We have no right to think that we have arrived, that we somehow deserve greater power. We are probably more off than on, more wrong than right, more in need of correction than commendation. And we haven't even talked about doctrine yet, about some of our miserably shallow, shamelessly man-serving, mutually contradictory teachings!

Of course, God is not demanding perfection. And He is a God who forgives. But sin still has ugly consequences. Our troubles will not just "go away." There must be a judgment first.

" I have forgiven them, as you asked, [the Lord replied to Moses, when he interceded for the Israelites after they refused to enter the Promised Land.] Nevertheless, as surely as I live and as surely as the glory of the Lord fills the whole earth, not one of the men who saw My glory and the miraculous signs I performed in Egypt and in the desert but who disobeyed Me and tested Me ten times — not one of them will ever see the land I promised on oath to their forefathers. No one who has treated Me with contempt will ever see it. But because My servant Caleb has a different spirit and follows Me wholeheartedly, I will bring him into the land he went to, and his descendants will inherit it" (Num. 14:20-24).

God grant us the spirit of Caleb. May we never treat the Lord with contempt!

We need to come humbly to the throne, to ask for mercy and grace — especially when it comes to the tragic lack of true holiness in our lives. We have really lost sight of the mark:

"As obedient children, do not conform to the evil desires you had when you lived in ignorance. But just as He who called you is holy, so be holy in all you do; for it is written, 'Be holy, because I am holy' " (1 Pet. 1:14-16).
We have seriously offended here. But the Lord in heaven will hear our prayer. He will honor a contrite heart.

"The Lord is close to the brokenhearted and saves those who are crushed in spirit" (Ps. 34:18).

"For this is what the high and lofty One says — He who lives forever, whose name is *holy*: 'I live in a high and *holy* place, *but also with him who is contrite and lowly in spirit*, to revive the spirit of the lowly and to revive the heart of the contrite' " (Is. 57:15).

He *will* restore His broken people.
He cannot go back on His Word.

He calls us to enter His holy place —
humbled and washed in the blood.

Chapter Eighteen

Restoring the Glory of God: Where Do We Go from Here?

Only a generation that has seen so little of the real outpouring of the Spirit could make such big boasts about almost nothing — singing about the army of the Lord and rejoicing in the victory of God while our nation staggers headlong toward destruction. Only a generation that has never experienced revival — in the fullest historic sense of the word — could use the word so lightly. Revival is marked by its *depth* — by the *quality* of the Spirit's presence, by an awesome fear of the Lord, by a terrible conviction of sin, by the recovery of the great themes of the cross and resurrection, by a marked increase in holiness, by a noticeable effect for good on the society at large, by *little children* weeping for their sins and being wonderfully transformed.

Deep repentance and true revival go hand in hand. We have not seen much deep repentance! During the Jesus movement in the early 1970's, large numbers of hippies worldwide were dramatically changed for life. They were radically transformed by a powerful move of the Lord. They repented from the depths of their heart. Yet for thousands of others, an alternative lifestyle that was better than drugs and immorality was discovered, but there was little brokenness for sin and hardly any understanding that the glorious God had been offended. And there was so much backsliding into the world by so many so quickly. Revival is more than this!

The Charismatic movement of the 1960's restored spiritual manifestations — and much spiritual life — to the traditional denominational churches. But for many, it only meant that a new experience was added *without recovering the character of God.* True revival always manifests the Lord!

There are some who claim that we could never have another city-wide or regional revival in the United States today, since our nuclear society tends to be so separated, on the move and independent. We hardly know our neighbors anymore. But all this will not stop the rapid spread of a blazing fire. Revival is marked by a supernatural working of the Spirit that is impossible to confine and that transcends human means. And, while genuine revival is *not* dependent on modern systems of communication or advanced media techniques, still — with all our televisions, radios, newspapers and magazines, and with telephones in virtually every home — a real revival could affect the whole nation overnight. Everybody would be talking. Millions would be turning.

The problem is not our modern social structure. The problem is our lack of fire.

For several straight decades the American Church has been on a steady decline in morals and integrity, family life and ethics, sacrifice and service. We have not been representing *Jesus.* How tragic it is that the more we succeed outwardly in the work of the Lord, the less we resemble inwardly the person of the Lord! All this must come to an abrupt halt *if we hope to see the glory of the Lord.*

The Holy Spirit has become distant from our meetings. James Edwin Orr points out that, in stark contrast to God's judgment on Ananias and Sapphira, believers today seem to "get away" with all kinds of deceptive or broken vows. "The fact that they have not suffered severely is evidence only of the longsuffering of God *in times of spiritual decline.*"

God's presence removed means God's judgment delayed. The more real God's presence is, the greater the immediate danger of judgment.

"The Lord spoke to Moses after the death of the two sons of Aaron who died when they approached the Lord. The Lord said to Moses: 'Tell your brother Aaron not to come whenever he chooses into the Most Holy Place behind the curtain in front of the atonement cover on the ark, or else he will die, because I appear on the cloud over the atonement cover' " (Lev. 16:1-2).
One wrong move could be fatal, because God's glory was literally there. Three more times similar warnings were given on the day of Nadab and Abihu's death (Lev. 10:6-8).

But centuries later, before King Josiah purged the Temple, it was filled with all kinds of idol worshippers, all sorts of unclean pagan priests, and whole guilds of homosexual prostitutes. Yet these violators weren't dropping dead. Fire from heaven didn't consume them like it consumed Nadab and Abihu. Why? Because God's presence had already departed. His vengeance was being stored up. It was about to come crashing down, and countless thousands of Jews were about to be butchered; the very Temple would be destroyed! *The book of Lamentations tells us exactly what to expect when horrible sins have been committed by the people of God and the divine axe has not fallen.*

It is frightening to see judgment delayed, since that means that judgment must be accumulating. *The American Church has yet to be fully judged for her enterprising idolatries and her worldly adulteries.* What a sobering thought! It would have been easier for us to have swiftly been dealt with than to have been allowed to go on in our dream world for so long. The end could really be awful. At the least, it will bring real pain. It is time for some profound change. Can Jesus begin with you and me? Here is a challenge for our day:

Our game-show gospel must end.

The unspoken — and most probably unconscious — philosophy of many of us has been: We want it all, as long as it costs us nothing! We are willing to make any sacrifice — as long as no hardship is involved. We will gladly persevere in faith — as long as it doesn't take too long. We want to bring God's purposes to birth — as long as there are no labor pains. In the world people wine and dine. In our "Spirit-filled" circles we worship and dine. This way of thinking must become a thing of the past. We need to adjust our mind set. It is time to consider our ways. In the Lord, *nothing* of real spiritual value comes cheap.

Prayer *and* fasting must be our portion. Discipline must become a way of life. (John Wesley woudn't ordain a man who didn't fast until dinner time two days a week.) We must learn to "afflict our souls" and recover the blessedness of mourning. Church meetings must become more than just one big celebration. Not *every* service needs to end on an upbeat note! We don't *always* have to leave happy. God never said, "You must constantly feel good!" He would rather we feel His heart. Sometimes even God grieves. Serving Him may be a great adventure, but it certainly was not meant to be fun and games. Let's "prepare [our] minds for action [and] be self-controlled" (1 Pet. 1:13). Times of great evil lie ahead. God's *army* must be equipped and trained. Then it can come forth.

A new breed of leaders must arise.

Many of today's prominent church leaders seem to be the spiritual equivalent of the rich and famous. They are the powerful manager-types, the big operators, the high-level gospel magnates. But is this the primary pattern for New Testament elders and ministers? Did Paul raise up executive pastors? Why does it seem that many of these men and women who are so "big" in the body could be equally big in the world *using the same principles and techniques?* Isn't God's kingdom based on very different laws?

A. W. Tozer was tragically correct when he said:
"A good personality and a shrewd knowledge of human nature is all that any man needs to be a success in religious circles today. [Like the world,] Christians have fallen into the habit of accepting the noisiest and most notorious among them as the best and the greatest. They too have learned to equate popularity with excellence, and in open defiance of the Sermon on the Mount they have given their approval not to the meek but to the self-assertive; not to the mourner but to the self-assured; not to the pure in heart who see God but to the publicity hunter who seeks headlines."
What is great in the eyes of man is often gross in the eyes of God.

Are we measuring success by earthly standards or by the standards of heaven?

"Better a little with the fear of the Lord than great wealth with turmoil. Better a meal of vegetables where there is love than a fattened calf with hatred" (Prov. 15: 16-17).

"Better a little with righteousness than much gain with injustice. Better a dry crust with peace and quiet than a house full of feasting, with strife" (Prov. 16:8, 17:1).

"Better one handful with tranquility than two handfuls with toil and chasing after wind" (Eccl. 4:6).

Ten choice servants are of more value to the Lord than ten thousand cheap showmen.

The ministry is not a business. Neither is it a political empire. There is a place for God-filled fishermen and tax-collectors. Brokenness and humility are a must. It is the poor in spirit who are blessed. The LORD is the source of their strength.

Personal ambition must be slaughtered on the altar. The superstar mentality of the "anointed elite" must be violently nailed to the cross. The only way up is down, and before we can stand and speak in public we must lay prostrate on our faces in private.

Our Master is our example:

"Jesus knew that the Father had put all things under His power, and that He had come from God and was returning to God; so He got up from the meal, took off His outer clothing, and wrapped a towel around His waist. After that, He poured water into a basin and began to wash His disciples' feet, drying them with the towel that was wrapped around Him" (John 13:3-5).

Because He knew exactly who He was, He could humble Himself into the dust. What an awesome display of authority!

"Now that I, your Lord and Teacher, have washed your feet, you should also wash one another's feet. I have set you an example that you should do as I have done for you. I tell you the truth, no servant is greater than his master, nor is a messenger greater than the one who sent him. Now that you know these things, you will be blessed if you do them" (John 13:14-17).

We need more selfless servants who are secure in their standing with God. Let the world fight for reputation and position. Let them have all the "honor" they want. We need only to please our Father. Let fleshly vindication die! Pride is the flip-side of insecurity. Those who know God's love can afford to put their defenses down. The Lord is their shield and their song.

"Perfect love will never want the preeminence in everything; it will never want to take the place of another; it will always be willing to take the back seat. At conventions there is always someone who wants to give a message, who wants to be heard. If you have a desire to go to a convention you should have three things settled in your mind. Do I want to be heard? Do I want to be seen? Do I want financial gain? If I have these things in my heart I have no right to be there. The one thing that must move us must be the constraining love of God to minister for Him" (Smith Wigglesworth).

This is the mark of leaders under God. They are constrained to serve and give with nothing selfish to gain, no worldy aspirations to fulfill, and no insecure egos to build. This is the Jesus pattern.

We must come to the end of all human agendas
and put no confidence in the flesh.

Moses didn't want to be the mighty deliverer of Israel. Elijah never wanted to be on Mount Carmel. Paul never dreamed of going to the Gentiles. That was why they were so greatly used! "For it is we who are the circumcision, [said Paul,] we who worship by the Spirit of God, who glory in Christ Jesus, and who put no confidence in the flesh — though I myself have reasons for such confidence" (Phil. 3:3-4). But he nailed those credentials to the cross. It was the anointing alone that accomplished the work. Paul understood this in full: "[God] has made us competent as ministers of a new covenant — not of the letter but of the Spirit; for the letter kills, but the Spirit gives life" (2 Cor. 3:6). Didn't Jesus make this absolutely clear? "I am the vine; you are the branches. If a man remains in Me and I in him, he will bear much fruit; *apart from Me you can do nothing*" (John 15:5).

Yet so much supposed ministry for the Lord is done apart from Him — apart from His direction, apart from His will, apart from His enabling. God says, "On your mark!" — and we're already off and running. He says, "Get set!" — but we're already down the track. By the time He says, "Go!" we're too far away to hear His voice anymore.

Most ministry today is either ahead of the Lord (the leaders have God's plan but not His timing), behind the Lord (God has moved on to something new and the leaders have not responded), outside of the Lord (what the leaders are doing may look good, but it has nothing to do with the will of God), or without the Lord (the leaders are following the plan of God without the power of God). This must change dramatically if we are ever to see a pure move of the Lord.

Moses prayed a prayer and the earth swallowed his foes. It was a breathtaking display of power and an awesome vindication of the servant of the Lord. But Moses was only following

God's plan. He was not a self-anointed leader with a self-appointed agenda: "This is how you will know that the Lord has sent me to do all these things and that it was not my idea" (Num. 16:28). If only we too could learn! "Your plan, Lord; not my ideas!"

Elijah called down fire from heaven in the presence of the crowds on Carmel. But this was the key to his strength: "O Lord, God of Abraham, Isaac and Israel, let it be known today that you are God in Israel and that I am Your servant and have done all these things *at Your command*" (1 Kin. 18:36). "All this at *Your* command! Lord, may *Your* name alone be exalted!" And when the fire fell, the people "fell prostrate and cried, 'The Lord — He is God! The Lord — He is God!' " (1 Kin. 18:39). To *Him* alone be the glory! May *His* kingdom come and *His* will be done — on this earth, in our hearts and in our heads. He will only bless the work He has called for. Why labor and toil in vain?

Look carefully at this amazingly detailed account of how God led Israel through the wilderness. Make sure you read every word!

"Whenever the cloud lifted from above the Tent, the Israelites set out; wherever the cloud settled, the Israelites encamped. At the Lord's command the Israelites set out, and at His command they encamped. As long as the cloud stayed over the tabernacle, they remained in camp. When the cloud remained over the tabernacle a long time, the Israelites obeyed the Lord's order and did not set out. Sometimes the cloud was over the tabernacle only a few days; at the Lord's command they would encamp, and then at His command they would set out. Sometimes the cloud stayed only from evening till morning, and when it lifted in the morning, they set out. Whether by day or by night, whenever the cloud lifted, they set out. Whether the cloud stayed over the tabernacle for two days or a month or a year, the Israelites would remain in camp and not set out; but when it lifted, they would set out. At the Lord's command they encamped, and at the Lord's command they set out. They obeyed the Lord's order, in accordance with His command through Moses" (Num. 9:17-23).

Can you imagine what this was like? The children of Israel were wandering around in a vast wilderness. Many times there was no apparent rhyme or reason to where, when or why the cloud moved or stopped. And it was a massive undertaking to dismantle the tabernacle, break camp, and march forward — especially when the people had become comfortable! "Why did the Lord stop *here*? Why couldn't we stay where we were? Why did we encamp for one day, only to move on the next? It makes absolutely no sense." God said: "Follow the cloud." He was teaching His people a lesson: "Don't move without My command." Marching forward without Him is presumption. Staying still when He moves is rebellion. Our only hope is to cling to His side. It is folly to move without the cloud. Yet sometimes we hate to wait!

What would have happened to the world if the 120 disciples in the upper room had become impatient and decided *not* to follow the Lord's command to *wait* for the Spirit's outpouring, and instead had begun to preach openly in Jerusalem without the anointing from on high? What a tragedy that would have been! But are *we* waiting for the Lord today, or are we running on fleshly fuel?

It has often been said that, "If the Spirit of God were to leave the earth today, 90% of all Christian ministry would continue unaffected." This certainly applies to the Church in North America! If so many of our leaders are hearing accurately from

God, if we are so closely adhering to His plan and charting His course, if we are not largely following our own burdens and pursuing our own goals, then why are we failing so miserably in making true disciples of Jesus and impacting our nation for Him? God's best word to some ministries and churches in our land might be, "Shut down!" How many are willing to hear that?

Leaders, stop and search your hearts. Are you using people to accomplish *your* purposes? Are you soliciting money to build *your* work? Are you willing to see the people leave and the funds dry up if God has something better for them — or different for you? Can you say you are doing *God's* work in *God's* way? Are you seeing *God's* results? (This is not always a matter of numbers. But if the Spirit is active in our midst He will bring lasting, vibrant fruit.) How many ministries today are living fossils? — the shell is there but the power is gone. Can we humble ourselves before God and cry out: "Your will, Lord, or nothing at all!" Why continue to preach a message or prop up a ministry or church that He is not in?

The Federal Drug Administration bans the distribution of all medicines that have not been clinically proven to work. How many of our "gospel cures" would be outlawed if they were quality tested too? How many ministers would be convicted of prescribing spiritual placebos to dying congregants? Man's answers and methods, even if they are baptized in prayer and sanctified with the Word, cannot remove the cancer of sin. Only God's work done in God's way can accomplish God's will. Nothing else makes sense. Nothing else will do. There are no acceptable substitutes for following the cloud alone.

God knows where He is going. Do we?

Chapter Nineteen

The All-Surpassing Exellence of the Gospel

No mortal voice can fully proclaim the gospel of grace. No human being can adequately declare the good news. The theme is too lofty, too sacred, too deep, too pure. We can only preach, compose, teach and write with the help of the Holy Spirit.

That's why Charles Wesley cried out:

> Oh for a thousand tongues to sing
> My great redeemer's praise,
> The glories of my God and King,
> The triumphs of His grace.

One tongue, one voice, one language was not enough, and never will be, to express our praise to God or our responsibility to man.

Wesley asked for the assistance of heaven:

> "My gracious Master and my God,
> Assist me to proclaim,

> To spread through all the earth abroad
> The honors of Thy name."

He asked the Lord to help him in proclaiming worldwide the honors of God's name. How we need fresh inspiration today! We have so many words with so little weight, so many preachers with so little power, so many minstrels with so little majesty.

Our educational standards are down. Our family and moral standards are down. We have dragged the gospel down too! We spoon-feed our listeners Bible pablum and cater our writing to an elementary school mentality. And while there is nothing wrong with simple teaching, some people refuse to think! Being spiritual does not require shutting off the mind; it requires renewing the mind. But we live in a society that has largely exchanged the art of contemplation and meditation for the science of calculators and computers!

When Harvard University (originally Harvard College) was founded here in 1636, students were required to be competent in Latin — able to read, write and speak Latin prose and verse "with tolerable skill and without assistance" as well as being grounded in Greek grammar *in order to be admitted to the school*. Once they were in, strict discipline was demanded:

> "No student must be absent from his studies or stated exercises for any reason (unless it is first made known to the President or a tutor, and by them approved) with the exception of the half-hour allowed for lunch, a half-hour for dinner and also for supper, until nine o'clock" (Cotton Mather).

And the university was not just a place of study. In fact, 300 years ago it was a more godly and reverential place than most American Christian *homes* are today! These are a few more of the early Harvard laws:

No student of any class, shall "visit any shop or tavern, to eat and drink, unless invited by a parent, guardian, stepparent, or some such relative";

"No student shall buy, sell or exchange any thing without the approval of his parents, guardians, or tutors";

"All students must refrain from wearing rich and showy clothing, nor must any one go out of the college-yard, unless in his gown, coat or cloak";

"No one must, under any pretext, be found in the society of any depraved or dissolute person" (Today depraved and dissolute persons teach at some of our colleges!);

"If any student shall, either through willfulness or negligence, violate any law of God or of this college, after being twice admonished, he shall suffer severe punishment, at the discretion of the President or his tutor. But in high-handed offences, no such modified forms of punishment need be expected."

In order to graduate from Harvard with the most basic degree in Arts (not Theology! — that came later), the student had to be able "logically to explain the Holy Scriptures, both of the Old and New Testaments ... and ... be blameless in life and character." Look at how things have changed!

Our college graduates now have more information at their finger tips, and probably less truth in their heads and holiness in their hearts, than any generation in American history. Our artificial intelligence has produced some very superficial people! This same disease has afflicted the Church: We have every kind of study Bible, language tool and easy learning aid. But we never want to really dig, so we have turned out a generation of shallow believers who thrive on surface thrills. *The gospel is so much deeper than this.*

Let's go back to England in the 1600's. There were few writers greater than John Milton. Yet, in spite of all his genius, when he began his classic work, *Paradise Lost*, he knew he was not equal to the task. How could he communicate the horror of Satan's fall, the agony of Adam's sin, the response of God the Son? Listen to Milton's lofty words of petition:

> Instruct me, for Thou knowst: Thou from the first
> Wast present ...
> What in me is dark
> Illumine, what is low raise and support
> That to the height of this great [subject]
> I may assert Eternal Providence,
> And justify the ways of God to Men.

We may not pray in such poetic words — God hears the prayer of the simple washwoman as much as He hears the prayers of the sophisticated writer — but have we shared Milton's heart? How often have we prayed prayers like his? "God, instruct me; illumine what is dark in me, and what is low, raise and support! Oh Lord, take me higher so that I may be worthy of declaring Your truth: the wonder of Your grace, the abundance of Your love, the greatness of Your power, the glory that is to come!" We need the touch of heaven. We need to be caught *up* in the Lord.

Listen to the words of the eighteenth century hymn writer Robert Robinson:

> Come Thou Fount of every blessing,
> Tune my heart to sing Thy grace;
> Streams of mercy, never ceasing,
> Call for songs of loudest praise.

> Teach me some melodious sonnet,
> Sung by flaming tongues above;
> Praise the mount — I'm fixed upon it —
> Mount of Thy redeeming love.

"Lord, tune *our* hearts to sing Your grace. Teach *us* a new song sung by flaming tongues above. Settle *us* on top of the mount of Your redeeming love. Show forth Your glory *through us!*"

No one had more experience and knowledge in preaching the gospel than the apostle Paul. Yet he still asked the Colossians to pray "that we may proclaim the mystery of Christ, for which I am in chains. *Pray that I may proclaim it clearly, as I should*" (Col. 4:3-4). He could never preach Jesus' riches on his own.

The psalmist declared: "My heart is stirred by a noble theme as I recite my verses for the king; my tongue is the pen of a skillful writer" (Ps. 45:1). Do we dare lift our voices to speak of the Lord without *our* hearts being stirred? Is the gospel any less noble today then it was in centuries past? Are *our* tongues like the pen of a skillful writer? Our pulpits boast many smooth speakers and sharp salesmen (not to mention smart seminarians), but how many of them penetrate the depths of the cross or the heights of the ascension? How much of their message is sublime? But the Word of God is sublime.

Smith Wigglesworth was an illiterate plumber. His wife taught him to read, and for life, the only book he read was the Bible. He was not widely read, but he read the Word widely. Wigglesworth was *deep* in the Lord. He taught that "God's Word is 1) supernatural in origin; 2) eternal in duration; 3) inexpressible in valour; 4) infinite in scope; 5) regenerative in power; 6) infallible in authority; 7) universal in application;

and 8) inspired in totality." He exhorted his hearers to: "Read it through; write it down; pray it in; work it out; pass it on ... The Word of God changes a man until he becomes an Epistle of God." We need to be *changed* by the Word.

We would do well to follow this example: "My heart grew hot within me, and as I meditated, the fire burned; *then* I spoke with my tongue" (Ps. 39:3). Then he had something worth saying. Then he had something worth hearing.

So much of our teaching and preaching today is just plain trivial. It hardly ever takes wing and soars. It is so mundane, so unexceptional, so tepid. It makes the Good News commonplace, casual and almost crass. It rarely adorns the Savior or graces the hearer. In fact, it even makes the gospel attainable by mere human effort. Yet salvation is beyond the grasp of man alone!

Of course, the gospel is totally and absolutely free. No one would argue with this. "The Spirit and the bride say, 'Come!' And let him who hears say, 'Come!' Whoever is thirsty, let him come; and whoever wishes, let him take the free gift of the water of life" (Rev. 22:17). What a glorious word! God forbid that anyone should ever minimize the amazing wideness of His grace. It is available for "whosoever will." But, without the intervention of God, it is totally unobtainable.

When Jesus taught that it was hard for those who have riches to enter the kingdom of God, the disciples were "amazed, and said to each other, 'Who then can be saved?' Jesus looked at them and said, 'With man this is impossible, but not with God; all things are possible with God' " (Mark 10:26-27). That is the heart of the gospel!

When the angel Gabriel announced to a startled young maiden that she, a virgin, would bear a Son by the power of the Spirit, his miraculous news didn't stop there: "Even Elizabeth your relative is going to have a child in her old age, and she who was said to be barren is in her sixth month. For nothing is impossible with God" (Luke 1:36-37).

Do you hear what the angel is saying? "Mary, this is a whole new order. With man it can't happen. Virgins do not have children; old women like Elizabeth do not conceive. But this is the gospel, Mary. Nothing will be impossible with God!" With Him the barren are blessed, and a virgin gives birth to the Savior of the world! What humanity could not accomplish in a billion ages and worlds, God performs in a moment. The gospel declares *wonderful* news.

Listen again to Charles Wesley, as he is carried along by the majesty of the Spirit and intoxicated by the ability of the Lord. He calls for something astounding:

"Hear Him, ye deaf; His praise, ye dumb,
Your loosened tongues employ;
Ye blind, behold your Savior come,
And leap, ye lame, for joy!"

How can the deaf *hear* the Lord, or the dumb *sing* His praise, or the blind *behold* their Savior, or the lame *leap* for joy? How can they be commanded to do what they cannot do? But that is the essence of the gospel! It is always impossible with man and only possible with God. We are helpless until we are helped by Him. This is what G. Campbell Morgan meant when he said: "When I attempt to do what I can't do, then I do it in the power of the Spirit." If we can accomplish the work entirely on our own, then it's not the work of the Lord.

The gospel is the power of God (Rom. 1:16). It is the gospel of the impossible. It tells dead men to rise and living men to die. It commands unbelievers to have faith and look at One they cannot see. And it urges selfish sinners to lose what they want to keep. The gospel takes the standards of this world and turns them upside down. It sees the victory of God in the crucifixion of His Son and tells us we are strong when we are weak. Who is worthy to bring this Word? Who is *able* to bring it?

When the gospel is truly preached it leaves men crying out for *salvation*. It makes them realize their utter *hopelessness*. It reveals to them the wonder of *grace*. It produces a thankful heart. When people hear the message and say, "Who then can be saved?" they may actually be understanding the Good News for the first time in their lives, even if they've heard it dozens of times before. And when Jesus is truly lifted up — when He is exalted as the blessed Savior and Redeemer, when our hearts warm to the marvel of His love, when our lips are brimming over with the proclamation of His triumph — then we are preaching the Word. He has come, He has died, He has risen! When we magnify the Lamb upon the throne, when we extol the Holy One who was slain, when we acclaim the Righteous Son of God, then we are in the Spirit and heaven overflows.

But today, what do we have? Where the gospel is not cold, as it often is in dead formalistic churches, it is sold — with hype, with flesh and with earthly means. Seldom has the Good News of Jesus ever been as diluted and polluted as it has been in our day and in our land. The gospel must be glorious, not gaudy; supernatural, not sensational. But we have dealt in dross for so long that we have mistaken it for silver. Most contemporary American believers have never seen the real product in its beauty. We have lost sight of the preciousness of the truth!

But the blessed gospel cannot be contained for ever. It cannot be held back much more. The wonder of the message is too great. It must burst the old wineskins (many so-called full-gospel/restorationist/cutting-edge/prophetic churches have more "old wineskins" than they know) and be poured out in full.

JESUS must be proclaimed!

We are the generation that has the possibility of reaching the entire world with the glorious word of redemption. We must walk worthy of this high call.

It would be tragic to demean the Lord anymore.

Chapter Twenty

A Radical Proposal?

"Every great historical personality is a revolutionary personality. As a result of his historical mission, he usually finds himself in strong conflict with his contemporaries. The more significant his mission, the greater is the conflict which continues to rage among the descendants until his mission is completed. What used to be revolutionary becomes an accomplished fact, a matter of course" (Dr. Isaac Breuer).

What was radical yesterday is regular today. But someone had to break with the crowd. Someone had to step out — even if it meant being misunderstood by his own generation. Someone had to be bold and seem like a fool in the eyes of many in order to make a fresh move. How we need holy radicals in our day! (Let me insert a word of warning here: The most radical thing some of us could do is nail our self-will, arrogance and unsubmissiveness to the cross. Before God can fully use obnoxious mavericks He must first break them down.)

The American Church is failing. Our society is crumbling. Foreigners are shocked when they visit our land. Our coins say, "In God we trust," but even our currency lies. When hostile Iranians call our country "The Great Satan," they are not entirely wrong. We have exported greed, smut and our own unique style of western worldliness to almost every nation on earth more successfully than we have exported the gospel and holy living. What an awful shame! *According to the testimony of our nation, Muslims and Marxists think Christianity is compromise.* Doesn't this break your heart?

According to a Gallup Poll released in the fall of 1990, 74% of our American people believe that they have made a personal commitment to Jesus. (95% of that number describe themselves as being born again.) Yet this statistic cannot possibly be true unless it is a different Jesus they are committed to, a different new birth they have experienced and a different message they have heard. Could these deceived multitudes be the direct products of our more fleshly televangelism? Are these "believers" some of the statistics we hear about weekly, as our superstar preachers assure us confidently that revival is in our land — or at least in their ministry? *Something in our churches must change.* It is time for holy radicals to arise.

Our nation has been more exposed to the "gospel" than has any other nation in the history of the world. But after several decades of nonstop preaching and teaching through countless thousands of radio and television broadcasts and innumerable books and tapes, this is where we stand today in the United States of America:

The leading cause of death for black males between the ages of 15 and 24 is *homicide.* Twenty-three percent of all black males in their twenties are either in jail or on probation or parole. *Two-thirds* of America's black children do not live with both of their parents.

Police with metal detectors stand guard at some of our high schools, and *elementary schools* are proud if they are drug free. Violent crime rose by 300% from 1960-1980, and in that same period of time, juvenile crime went up by *11,000%*. That was as of 1980. Those were the good old days!

In some schools, it is legal to pass out and recommend condoms to the teenage students, and *illegal* to distribute Bibles and gospel tracts. Teachers can talk freely about homosexuality and Planned Parenthood can boldly recommend incest (*five million* booklets that contain such trash were distributed to our kids), but try to proclaim Jesus clearly in our public schools and you may find yourself locked up.

"Twenty to 30 percent of college-age women are currently estimated to have genital herpes, a disease from which they will suffer the rest of their lives" (Dr. James Dobson). Twenty-nine percent of our 15-year-old girls and 72% of our 17-year-old boys are sexually active.

Operation Rescue workers peacefully protesting the murder of innocent babies have been harshly beaten *by local police*. (Thank God there are godly officers also.) Angry policemen have snapped rescuers' bones in two and dragged older men and women on their faces across the pavement, with the judges often backing this brutality.

A pro-life attorney was sentenced to 290 days in jail for contempt of court. His crime? Asking trial witnesses questions like, "Officer, were you once an unborn baby?"; or, to an abortionist, "How do you feel about making a living off the blood of babies?" For this he was judged a criminal by our contemporary "justice" system. What has happened to "the land of the free and the home of the brave"?

But this is what our culture has come to after forty years of day and night "gospel" preaching. It is clear that something in our message, something in our method, something in our ministries must radically change or history (and heaven) will call us a failure. So much opportunity has been given to us in this generation; so little has been done by us for our land. May God give us grace to awake.

Over 400 years ago, William Tyndale had an impossible dream, and for this he was persecuted and killed. He believed that the Scriptures should be made available in the language of the people (*that* was the "dangerous" position he held!). He gave himself sacrificially to the difficult task — having to flee his native England and hide out in Germany in order to continue translating — and was martyred by the traditional bigots of his day. He was strangled and burned at the stake!

Now, throughout the civilized world, all of us have the Scriptures in our native tongue. The Bible, in whole or in part, has been translated into more than 3,000 languages and dialects. True believers everywhere thank God for this. But when Tyndale — and John Wyclif before him — began to promote this work, they were rejected, ridiculed and rebuked. What an amazing fact. Those who were reviled yesterday as heretics by the traditional religious establishment are revered today as heroes!

We must take this lesson to heart. Some of *us* need to break with the mold if the mold has fossilized and died. *We* need to depart from tradition if tradition has departed from the truth. Let God's holy remnant arise, in meekness and dependence on the Lord.

When George Whitefield and the Wesley brothers experienced new birth in the 1700's, they came to an obvious conclusion: They must declare this new life in the churches. But most of the clergy were still dead in their sins; they didn't want such preaching in their midst. So a preposterous proposal was born: Whitefield decided to preach outdoors! Even John Wesley was shocked:

"It is a *mad* notion," he said. (Wesley admitted later that, "I should have thought the saving of souls almost a sin if it had not been done in a church.") But young George Whitefield prayed through, stepped out, and opened up his mouth — outdoors. Soon tens of thousands were being saved. Revival was aflame in the land! And it was that very same John Wesley who years later could say, "*The world* is my parish." What seemed so radical yesterday appears so regular today!

Everyone is waiting for someone else to do something. (That means someone is waiting for you!) No one wants to be the first to step out. We are afraid of what people will say. We don't want to rock the boat — even if the boat is sinking! Could this be what's holding us back? We will never accomplish God's will as long as our eyes are on men. Peer pressure smothers and stifles. Peer pressure lulls us to sleep. Peer pressure kills and constricts.

Listen to Catherine Booth:

"I believe it will be found, in the great day of account, that there have been more blessed enterprises squashed, more leadings of the Holy Ghost disobeyed, more urgings of the Spirit quenched, through the influence of what are called Christian friends than all other influences put together."

Let us be influenced by the Lord God instead!

We don't need any new "revelations"; the Scriptures alone are our source. We don't need any independent rebels; God is looking for servants who submit. But someone, somewhere, somehow must step out. Someone must make the first move.

We must recover the purity and simplicity of the gospel. Who will lead us back to the Word? It's all there if only we will search. THE TRUTH will shine forth as a light.

Almost one hundred years ago, Charles Parham started a Bible school in Topeka, Kansas. He called for mature believers from throughout the country to join him in the study of the Word. They were to live entirely by faith, selling their possesions before they came.

Soon a small group had joined him. They began to pour through the Scriptures. They examined the baptism in the Spirit. They saw how tongues were for today. Independently, they reached their conclusions. They were amazed to see that the others agreed. The only thing left to do was pray — and they prayed until God's power came down. On January 1, 1901, they were immersed in the Holy Spirit and began to speak in new tongues. And so the modern Pentecostal outpouring was birthed. But there was conception and travail first. Someone had to persevere and break through. Someone must break through today.

We must learn once again what it means to be holy. We must become truly separated saints. We must regain true purity and righteousness. Who will help set the example? Who will live out the standard of God? Let mockery and misunderstanding come. The Lord will stand at our side.

We must rediscover the meaning of sacrifice. We must remember we're just passing through. (This is *so* hard for us to grasp as Americans. Humanism and materialism have really had their sway!) Who will bring us an eternal perspective? We will *forever* be in fellowship with Jesus. Who will point us back to the Way? Who will direct us to the Author and Perfecter of our faith?

Our families are perishing in compromise and corruption. We have almost no idea how far we have fallen. Who will recover the home? Who will teach us what we have never been taught?

We have become so introspective and self-centered. We want more inner-healing and deliverance. But we have largely forgotten the needs of the *lost*. We must take our message from the confines of our cozy church buildings to the sinners who are dying on our streets. Who will help turn us inside out? Who will mobilize this great slumbering Church?

We need new heroes for a new generation. Who will leave all and set the pace? We need mothers and fathers, college students and professors, maids and garbage collectors, intellectuals and illiterates, young people and old people who will discover afresh what it means to follow Jesus. We need to take up the cross!

God is calling for men and women who will only do what they see their Father doing. He is calling for those who will set the Lord always before them, who will be caught up in the purpose of heaven and live out the message they preach. He is calling for holy disciples, wholly sold out and committed to His Son. He is fashioning a new kind of vessel — a vessel prepared for the glory of God!

How pitiful it is that with all our teaching, all our gifts and all our accomplishments we are still deformed, misshapen and warped. Could it be that today's Church needs reformation as much as the Church in Luther's day needed upheaval and change? Could it be that today's Church needs renewal and rehabilitation as much as the Church in Wesley's day needed to be totally transformed? Is this really such a revolutionary idea? Is this really such an extreme position? Is this really such a radical proposal?

It is up to you to decide — and once you decide you must act. God alone knows what the implications could be if you stand up, if you hear, if you obey.

The world will never be the same.

References

Page 11—For information on the "Healing Revival" of 1947-1958, see David Edwin Harrell, Jr., *All Things Are Possible: The Healing and Charismatc Revivals in Modern America* (Indiana University Press, 1975) and Richard M. Riss, *A Survey of 20th-Century Revival Movements in North America* (Hendricksen, 1988).

Page 20—A. W. Tozer, *Born After Midnight* (Christian Publications, 1989), p. 22.

Page 26—Dallas Willard, *The Spirit of the Disciplines* (Harper and Row, 1988), xii.

Pages 26-31—The account of Oswald Chambers' spiritual breakthrough is taken from Edwin and Lillian Harvey, *They Knew Their God*, Vol. 3 (Harvey and Tait, 1988), pp. 95-96.

Pages 29-30—A. W. Tozer, *Born After Midnight*, p. 8.

Pages 33-35—John Pollock, *George Whitefield and the Great Awakening* (Lion Publishing, 1972), pp. 164-166; for the complete unedited text of Nathan Cole's account (grammatical errors, misspellings and all), see Arnold Dallimore, *George Whitefield*, Vol. 1 (Banner of Truth, 1970), p. 542.

Page 36—*The Journals of George Whitefield* (repr., Banner of Truth, 1989), p. 479.

Pages 36-37—A. Skevington Wood, *The Burning Heart. John Wesley Evangelist* (Bethany, 1978), pp. 111-112.

Page 37—W. H. Fitchett, cited by Wood, *The Burning Heart*, p. 153, my emphasis.

Pages 38-39—E. Morgan Humphreys, cited by Emyr Roberts, *Revival and its Fruit,* with R. Geraint Gruffydd (Evangelical Library of Wales, 1981), p. 8.

Page 39—*The Life of Faith* account of the Stephen Jeffreys' meetings was cited by Colin C. Whittaker, *Seven Pentecostal Pioneers* (Gospel Publishing House, 1985), pp. 48-49.

Page 40—D. Martyn Lloyd Jones, *Joy Unspeakable. Power and Renewal in the Holy Spirit,* ed. Christopher Catherwood (Harold Shaw, 1984), p. 119.

Pages 41-42—Martyn Lloyd Jones, *Joy Unspeakable,* pp. 126-127.

Pages 43-44—For statistics on mass evangelism, see Ray Comfort, *Hell's Best Kept Secret* (Whitaker, 1989).

Page 46—For a detailed study of the key Hebrew word for healing, see my article on *rapha'* in the *Theologisches Wörterbuch zum Alten Testament,* ed. G. Johannes Botterweck and Helmer Ringgren, Vol. 7 (Kohlhammer, 1991), cols. 617-625 (the English version will be published by Eerdmans); and my book *Israel's Divine Healer* (forthcoming, 1992).

Page 47—C. Everett Koop, in *The Agony of Deceit,* ed. Michael Horton (Moody, 1990), p. 178. The complete sentence of Dr. Koop reads as follows: "Sickness is often the *proof* of God's special favor, and it always, in His loving pleasure, is coordinated with everything else that befalls the believer to achieve ultimately positive goals (Romans 8:28)."

Page 51—Jonathan Edwards, *Jonathan Edwards on Revival* (repr., Banner of Truth, 1987), pp. 90-91.

Page 51—For recent discussion of Paul's thorn, see Ralph P. Martin, *2 Corinthians,* Word Biblical Commentary (Word, 1986), pp. 411-418.

Page 52—F. F. Bosworth, *Christ the Healer* (Revell, 1973), p. 211.

Page 53—John G. Lake, *The John G. Lake Sermons on Dominion over Demons, Disease and Death,* ed. Gordon Lindsay (repr., Christ for the Nations, 1982), p. 68.

Page 58—Oswald Chambers, *Oswald Chambers. The Best from All His Works*, ed. Harry Verploegh, Vol. 1 (Oliver Nelson, 1987), p. 289. (Complete bibliographical references can be found there.)

Page 61—Paris Reidhead, *Getting Evangelicals Saved* (Bethany, 1989), p. 16.

Page 61—Carl F. Henry, *The Twilight of a Great Civilization*, cited in Reidhead, *Getting Evangelicals Saved*, p. 17.

Page 61—J. Edwin Orr, *My All, His All* (International Awakening Press, 1989), pp. 7-8.

Page 62—Richard Owen Roberts, *Revival* (Tyndale, 1988), p. 20.

Page 62—A. W. Tozer, *That Incredible Christian* (Christian Publications, 1986), pp. 23, 25.

Pages 70-73—Maria Woodworth-Etter, *Diary of Signs and Wonders* (repr., Harrison House, N.D.), pp. 107 (my emphasis), 72-73, 243 (my emphasis), 64-65, 142, 143 (my emphasis), 117, 346 (my emphasis).

Page 73—For the account of the witch doctor's deliverance, see *Only Love Can Make a Miracle. The Mahesh Chavda Story*, Mahesh Chavda with John Blattner (Servant, 1990), pp. 128-129.

Pages 75-76—A. W. Tozer, *Born After Midnight*, p. 33.

Page 76—Francis Frangipane, *Holiness, Truth and the Presence of God* (Advancing Church Publications, 1989), p. 65.

Page 77—John G. Lake, *Sermons*, p. 41.

Page 77—David Wilkerson, "Your Faith is Going into the Fire" (February 5, 1990), p. 1.

Pages 79-80—John G. Lake, *The New John G. Lake Sermons*, ed. Gordon Lindsay (repr., Christ for the Nations, 1981), pp. 29-30 (my emphasis).

Page 80—I was in Richmond, Virginia April 18-20 of 1986 and spoke directly to pastors who were involved in the early morning intercession meetings.

Page 82—G. Campbell Morgan, *The Westminster Pulpit*, Vol. II (Baker, repr., N.D.) pp. 20-21.

Page 86—The famous words, "the pen is mightier than the sword" were written by Edward George Bulwer-Lytton (Baron Lytton).

The entire quote is: "Beneath the rule of men entirely great, The pen is mightier than the sword" (*Richelieu*, II.ii).

Page 87—Moody Stuart, cited by David M. MacIntrye, *The Hidden Life of Prayer* (repr., Christian Literature Crusade, 1989), p. xvi.

Page 90—For the quotes of Coleridge and Jacob Boehme, as well David MacIntyre's own words, see MacIntyre, *Hidden Life*, p. 20.

Pages 91-92—Charles Finney, *Lectures on Revivals of Religion* (repr., Revell, N.D.), p. 58.

Page 92—David MacIntyre, *Hidden Life*, p. 75.

Page 92-93—Charles Finney, *Lectures on Revivals*, p. 89.

Page 93—Catherine and William Booth, *They Said It. William and Catherine Booth* (Salvationist Publishing, 1978), p. 32.

Page 99—For the Jackie Pullinger story, see *Chasing the Dragon*, Jackie Pullinger with Andrew Quicke (Servant, 1980).

Pages 103, 110, 112-114, 116—The quotations of Ambrose, Thomas Carlyle, Josh Billings, Bonnel Thornton, Lorenzo Dow, William James and Eugenie de Guerin are taken from *12,000 Religious Quotations*, ed. Frank S. Mead (repr., Baker, 1989), pp. 375-378; for the Oswald Chambers quotes, see *The Best of Oswald Chambers*, Vol. 1, pp. 288, 289, 287.

Page 104—William C. Burns, *Revival Sermons* (repr., Banner of Truth, 1980), p. 80.

Page 110—William Gurnall, *The Christian in Complete Armor* (repr., Banner of Truth, 1987), p. 13.

Page 111—Thomas Watson, *The Ten Commandments* (repr., Banner of Truth, 1987), pp. 206-207.

Page 111—A. W. Tozer, *Man: The Dwelling Place of God* (Christian Publications, 1966), p. 102.

Pages 113-114—John Trapp, quoted in *A Puritan Golden Treasury*, ed. I. D. E. Thomas (Banner of Truth, 1989), p. 238.

Page 114—Thomas Watson, *The Doctrine of Repentance* (repr., Banner of Truth, 1987), pp. 16-17.

Page 117—William C. Burns, *Revival Sermons*, p. 19.

Page 119—Francis Frangipane, "The Spirit of God's Kingdom," River of Life Ministries Newsletter, Vol. 4, No. 6 (1990) p. 1.

Pages 119-120—Smith Wigglesworth, cited from W. Hacking, *Smith Wigglesworth Remembered* (Harrison House, 1981), pp. 78, 101, 83.

Page 120—Isaac Ambrose, *Looking Unto Jesus* (repr., Sprinkle Publications, 1986), pp. 21, 19.

Page 120—Samuel Rutherford, *The Letters of Samuel Rutherford*, ed. Andrew Bonar (repr., Banner of Truth, 1984), p. 400.

Pages 122-123—John G. Lake, *Spiritual Hunger and Other Sermons*, ed. Gordon Lindsay (repr., Christ for the Nations,), pp. 45-46.

Page 123—A. W. Tozer, *Born After Midnight*, p. 13.

Pages 123-124—William C. Burns, *Revival Sermons*, pp. 21-22.

Page 130—Samuel Rutherford, *Letters*, p. 29.

Page 137—Robert Murray M'Cheyne, *Robert Murray M'Cheyne. Memoirs and Remains*, ed. Andrew Bonar (repr., Banner of Truth, 1966), p. 282.

Page 141—William C. Burns, *Revival Sermons*, p. 81.

Pages 141-142—The story of Gladys Aylward is taken from Ruth Tucker, *From Jerusalem to Irian Jaya* (Zondervan, 1983), pp. 249-254, where Alan Burgess, *The Small Woman*, is also quoted (see p. 251).

Page 143—A. Skevington Wood, *The Burning Heart*, p. 119.

Pages 143-145—John Lake's words to his workers are recounted in "The Unpublished Articles of John G. Lake," ed. Wilford H. Reidt, pp. 162-164, from the sermon entitled "Trumpet Call."

Page 145—Ignatius, quoted in *The Wisdom of the Saints*, ed. Jill Haak Adels (Oxford, 1987), p. 77.

Page 145—The words of Bishop Hugh Latimer can be found in *Foxes Book of Martyrs*, ed. W. Grinton Berry (Baker, 1989), p. 309.

Page 146—Richard Wurmbrand, "The Voice of the Martyrs," October, 1990, p. 3. ("The Voice of the Martyrs" is the monthly newsletter of Christian Missions to the Communist World.)

Pages 152-153—"Take Me into the Holy of Holies," written by Dave Browning (Copyright 1986, Glory Alleluia Music).

Page 159—James Edwin Orr, *My All, His All*, pp.45-46 (my emphasis).

Page 161—A. W. Tozer, *Born After Midnight*, p. 59; *Man: The Dwelling Place of God*, pp. 96-97.

Page 163—Smith Wigglesworth, *Ever Increasing Faith* (rev. ed., Gospel Publishing House, 1971), pp. 145-146.

Pages 170-171—Cotton Mather, *Magnalia Christi. The Great Works of Christ in America*, Vol. 2 (repr., Banner of Truth, 1979), pp. 24-25.

Pages 173-174—Jack Hywell-Davies, *The Life of Smith Wigglesworth* (Vine Books, 1988), p. 83.

Page 175—G. Campbell Morgan, quoted in Rosalind Goforth, *Jonathan Goforth* (Bethany, 1986), p. 135.

Page 179—Dr. Isaac Breuer, quoted in Jacob Breuer's Introduction to Rabbi Samson Raphael Hirsch, *The Nineteen Letters*, trans. Rabbi Dr. Bernard Drachman (Feldheim, 1969), pp. 10-11.

Page 180—The statistics regarding Black Americans are taken from *Newsweek*, October 15, 1990, p. 67.

Page 181—For the truth about Planned Parenthood, see George Grant, *Grand Illusions. The Legacy of Planned Parenthood* (Wolgemuth & Hyatt, 1988).

Page 181—Dr. James Dobson, *Focus on the Family* Magazine, November 1990, p. 4.

Page 181—The pro-life attorney sentenced to 290 days in jail was Cyrus Zal. See "Rescue Report," Aug/Sept 1990, p. 3.

Page 183—John Wesley, quoted in Pollock, *George Whitefield and the Great Awakening*, pp. 76-77.

Page 183—Catherine Booth, *The Writings of Catherine Booth. Papers on Godliness* (The Salvation Army, 1986), p. 43.

Page 184—For the Charles Parham story, see Gordon Lindsay, *They Saw it Happen!* (repr., Christ for the Nations, 1980), pp. 3-13.

Dialogue, Discussion and Debate:

Dr. Michael L. Brown and the Rabbis

ICN Ministries offers exciting and eye-opening videotapes and audiotapes of Dr. Brown's debates with leading rabbis and anti-missionaries.

These tapes are excellent for edification, education and outreach. Watch them, listen to them, and give them out!

For further information, contact ICN Ministries, P.O. Box 7355, Gaithersburg, MD 20898; call 301-990-4303, fax 301-990-4306, or E-mail: RevivalNow@msn.com.

In-Depth Self-Study Courses!

Choose from three courses specially prepared by Dr. Michael L. Brown.

Answering Jewish Objections to Jesus. This 12-tape series asks hard questions and provides solid, sound and scholarly answers. Ideal for all those involved in Jewish outreach and witnessing. Also excellent for those who have been confused by the anti-missionaries. The course comes with study guide and texts. (Dr. Brown's in-depth book on the subject of answering Jewish objections to Jesus will be available in the spring of 1997.)

The Messiah in Jewish Tradition. Learn the many, varied Jewish beliefs about the Messiah, from the Dead Sea Scrolls to the Talmud, from the Bible to Jewish mysticism. A fascinating, firsthand encounter with the ancient and medieval writings. Twelve tapes with textbook and study guide.

I Am the Lord Your Healer. This in-depth, faith-building teaching will help lay solid foundations of the Word in your life. Based on a careful study of the Hebrew and Greek, this comprehensive and practical course can easily be understood by any interested believer. Sixteen tapes, a study guide and Dr. Brown's full-length study *Israel's Divine Healer* are included.

Available through ICN Ministries, P.O. Box 7355, Gaithersburg, MD 20898; call 301-990-4303, fax 301-990-4306, or E-mail: RevivalNow@msn.com.

Are You Ready for Revival?

Dr. Michael L. Brown's stirring new book, *From Holy Laughter to Holy Fire: America on the Edge of Revival*, is must reading for all those hungry for the "real thing"—a glorious, heaven-sent, nation-shaking revival. The time is at hand!

In this penetrating, challenging and inspiring study, Dr. Brown reveals the roots of religious hypocrisy and manmade tradition that stand in the way of a national moving of the Spirit, urging believers to arise from spiritual slumber and theological pride before it's too late. He also confronts some of our entertainment-oriented, shallow, charismatic sensationalism, calling for a return to powerful preaching of holiness accompanied by deep conviction of sin. With constant examples drawn from past revivals, he outlines the chief characteristics of a true visitation, dealing also with the controversial questions of physical manifestations. And in no uncertain terms, he explains how genuine revival must make a radical impact on society. He challenges us to abandon our comfortable religion and dive in to uncompromising obedience to God in the fullness of the Spirit.

Is America on a collision course with revival, judgment, or both? How can we be ready? Read this book and find out!

(*From Holy Laughter to Holy Fire: America on the Edge of Revival* is an expanded edition of *High-Voltage Christianity*, originally published by Huntington House in 1995.)

Available at your local Christian bookstore or directly through ICN Ministries, P.O. Box 7355, Gaithersburg, MD 20898; call 301-990-4303, fax 301-990-4306, or E-mail: RevivalNow@msn.com.